This book must be returned or renewed on or before th

VERITAS FAMILY RESOURCES

ONE FLESH

by

FATHER CHUCK GALLAGHER S.J.

CATHOLIC COMMUNICATIONS INSTITUTE
DUBLIN
1980

First published March 1980 by
Veritas Family Resources,
7-8 Lr. Abbey St.,
Dublin 1, Ireland.

Acknowledgement

Scripture quotations are from the Jerusalem Bible published and © 1966, 1967
and 1968 by Darton, Longman & Todd Ltd., and Doubleday & Co. Inc. and
are used by permission of the publishers.

Designed by Liam Miller
Cover by Bill Bolger

Nihil obstat:
Richard Sherry, D.D.,
Censor deputatus.

Imprimi potest:
+ Dermot,
Archbishop of Dublin,
17 March, 1980.

The *nihil obstat* and *imprimatur* are a declaration that a text is considered to
be free of doctrinal or moral error. They do not necessarily imply agreement
with opinions expressed by the author.

ISBN 0-905092-96-1
Origination by Healyset, Dublin.
Printed and bound in the Republic of Ireland by Genprint Ltd., Dublin 3.

CONTENTS

*To all the couples
who have opened my eyes
to who the Church is.*

I

LOOKING FOR THE WAY

All of us agree today that the Church is in trouble all over the world. Certainly knowledgeable people in Europe have been talking for decades about the de-Christianisation of the population. Ever since Vatican II we in the Church have become more and more aware of the deep underlying malaise that has existed for a long time, but we have only begun to recognise it recently. We can put a lot of reasons on it, people can analyse it to death, but the basic fact of the matter is that people are having more and more difficulty with the Church.

People, of course, have always had a difficulty with the Church, right from the beginning. Faith after all is a gift. Furthermore, the Church expects a lot of us, so there has always been not only a problem in accepting the mission of the Church and the truth and beauty of the Church but also in living up to what it expects of us.

However, what we're experiencing in today's Church is quite different. It is very good and sincere and faithful people who are having the difficulties now, people who in times past would have been our backbone. People who have received the Sacraments for years, people who have been exposed to Catholic education practically all of their lives are turning down the Church — or at least, are very reluctant to get too involved in the Church. Many people are still going to Church, but their heart is really not in it. They are going because they have always gone or because they don't want to let their parents down or because they have a sense of guilt when they don't go or because they judge that some religion is good for their children — therefore, they should give them good example.

If we were to look at an overview of people in the Church, it would seem that they fall into one of several broad groups, all wanting to loosen their ties with the Church, not wanting to be too identified as Catholic.

One group believes that we have to get away from denominations; it is just the Lord that counts and we have to allow the Lord to take over our lives. The Church, then, at best, fits into the periphery of that relationship with Jesus. Theirs tends to be a rather passive experience of Church. Naturally, there is some real truth in this — good people don't do bad things; Jesus really is the Lord and our whole way of life has to revolve around him. But their relationship is too much with a disembodied Jesus, leaving out the dimension of the community of love, the Church he has established to be the prime way we express our relationship with him. They have found the Lord in *isolation* from his people and they are happy enough with fellowship. Jesus offers his Body and they settle for fellowship — an association of good people who have had a common experience.

Another group makes Jesus a good religious teacher who has good ideas and good norms to follow. For them, the real thing is having humanistic ideals and taking care of people. Once again, the Church fits in, insofar as it follows those ethical norms and insofar as it advances the course of social justice, peace, etc. Such an approach enables people to stand outside the Church and to judge her. It makes our relationship with the outside world more important than our relationship with one another. It calls for us to relate to people not in terms of their personhood, but in terms of some external circumstances such as poverty, need, hurt, oppression, etc.

Such people frequently have deep personal relationships and involvement with people who share their light and their vision. The difficulty is that so many of these communities are without the Lord. They may very definitely be real believers in the Lord, but it's a Lord who is a director of social ministry rather than a Lord who calls them to belong to one another and to let the compassion for others come out of that belonging.

A third group has just a great deal of indifference; they have retreated into their own little world of taking care of their own interests. Probably the vast majority of people in the Church today, certainly the practising people, would fall into this category. Their morale is low; they are confused and directionless. They don't know whom they can trust in the Church. As a result they have withdrawn and become for all practical purposes practising non-believers. They do the right Catholic things the appropriate number of times, but their hearts are unconverted. They have settled just to live their own lives, to get ahead and satisfy themselves. People who have degenerated into that kind of state have not done so of their own free choice; they simply see no other option. They see the Church as calling them to some other-worldliness, either in terms of a disembodied spirituality or an idealistic do-goodism. The choices offered them are so exacting and narrow that their hope and vision is limited and lifeless.

Attempts to renew the Church and change this whole situation, however, usually start at the wrong end. We examine what is wrong with the official Church, instead of looking at what people are saying, what they are looking for, what they need and what they are expressing as their desires. After all, it is the baptised people that are the Church. Too often we look at philosophies and theologies rather than the experience of the faithful. We have just got to start with the people. Unless we speak to them in their language, we are never going to be heard, because we are just talking abstractions.

Unfortunately, in just looking at the institutional Church, and seeing what changes have to be made there, we overlook the fact that the basic problem in the Church is not the institution. Much more important is to look at what our relationship is with one another and who we discern ourselves to be. This is not to say that the institution doesn't have to be changed and changed drastically, but we could have the world's most perfect institution within the framework of the Church, and that will not fundamentally change the way people react to the Church. The change in the Church has to be much more radical than trying to revise our theologies, our canon laws, our parish structures and so on. It is the society itself, the people of the Church, that is going to have to change.

This is not to suggest, then, that structural changes have no relevance at all. Great changes obviously have to be made, not simply because the structures are inadequate in themselves and frequently positively harmful, but more importantly because they

11

are a symbol of how we have depersonalised one another as Church and reduced our being Catholic to function and practice. But they are really not the main point. That is not facing into what the general population of the world is saying to us.

They are saying fundamentally that we are irrelevant, that they don't at all see the Church as adding an extra dimension to their lives. They don't see the Church as putting any fresh meaning into life. They don't see the Church as bringing anything to them that they don't already have.

No, changing the structures is not the answer. We just have to look around for some other way to make the Church vital, different and meaningful in today's society.

In addition to looking to people we need to look to Scripture. For Scripture tells us what that way is. The Bible makes it very clear to us how the Church is to be revealed:

"Husbands should love their wives just as Christ loved the Church and sacrificed himself to her to make her holy. He made her clean by washing her in water with a form of words, so that when he took her to himself she would be glorious, with no speck or wrinkle, or anything like that, but holy and faultless. In the same way husbands must love their wives as they love their own bodies; for a man to love his wife is for him to love himself. A man never hates his own body, but he feeds it and looks after it, and that is the way Christ treats the Church, because it is his body, and we are its living parts. For this reason, a man must leave his father and mother and be joined to his wife, and the two will become one body. This mystery has many implications, but I am saying it applies to Christ and the Church. To sum up, you too, each one of you, must love his wife as he loves himself, and let every wife respect her husband."

St. Paul is stating very clearly and bluntly that the way the community of believers, the Church, is loved by Jesus is revealed by the way husbands and wives in the Church relate to one another. So consequently the Church has to work on that. We have to examine and see clearly just how our Catholic husbands and wives are revealing the relationship of Jesus and the Church.

We are to be a community of love. That's what the Church is.

We, these believing people, are to be a community, are to belong to one another with him as our head.

Even in human terms, this makes a great deal of sense. The whole world is screaming for community. Everybody admits the need for community — from sociologists and academicians down to the normal man on the street. No one can deny the tremendous heartfelt need for closeness, roots, involvement in the lives of others, and for a caring community. We all want to care for others and be cared for by others.

And that is what is held out by Jesus. That is what the Church is all about — to bring alive the statement of Jesus that we are to love one another as he has loved us.

But in order to understand this community of love we are called to be, we have to get back to St. Paul's great mystery. That is our bedrock — that the way a husband loves his wife reveals how Jesus loves the Church. We need to look to Matrimony. We need to examine it and see that our married people understand their own significance.

One of our problems, though, is that we don't have an adequate understanding of any vocation, never mind the vocation of Matrimony. We keep mixing career and vocation. For example, we make being a doctor or a lawyer or a teacher a vocation. It's not — it's a career, and a very good and very beautiful career that offers the possibility of a high level of service in accordance with the Gospel. But service (or ministry) looms too large in our consciousness. It takes too big a place in our understanding of what being Gospel is. We think the prime, almost exclusive mission Jesus Christ has called us to, is one of *service* rather than one of *love,* or to be more fair about it, we've equated love with service.

Service can be and frequently is an *expression* of the love that exists between people, but the real love is the *relationship* we establish with one another and that is only *symbolised* by what we do for one another.

Really, there are only four vocations in the Church: Matrimony, Dedicated Single Life, Religious Life and Priesthood. Each one of these vocations is a unique way to love within the faith family. The fact is that a vocation doesn't focus on what we do. It's a call to a specific relationship to the rest of the faithful. It is this

13

relationship with the people of the Church that is our call and it is this we have to spend out life to establish.

How we exercise our talents can be our career. It might be as a librarian, a teacher, a director of religious education, a counsellor, a social worker or what have you. Career or profession, then, concerns itself with ministry. Whereas vocation concerns itself with way of life. Fundamentally, being a member of the Church is to commit myself to a way of life.

All too often, however, we look on vocation in terms of what we do: What do I do as a priest? What do I do as a sister? What do I do as a committed baptised-confirmed person? But that's the second question. The first question and the basic one for the adult in the Church is: What fundamental relationship am I going to have with the people of God? As a celibate in Orders? As a celibate in community? As a married person? As a celibate lay person?

Only then can I ask myself: "How am I going to spend that relationship in your midst? How am I going to spend my marriage? My Orders? My community? How am I going to express, in concrete terms, my relationship with my fellow believers? Whether that relationship is direct, such as priesthood, or indirect, such as marriage or religious life.

And when we grasp this idea of vocation, then we can begin to approach an understanding of the Sacrament of Matrimony and therefore of the Church.

It is only by understanding the Sacrament of Matrimony, in fact, that we can start to understand the Church. For in the case of both, what we're talking about is *people,* not structures, not activities, not institutions, not rituals. When we talk about the Sacrament of Matrimony we're talking about the sacramental couple; when we're talking about Church we're talking about this specific community of believers, this faith people. In no way are we trying to deny that the hierarchy and organisation and structure are part of this whole thing, but the Church in essence is these specific faithful people in their relationship to one another in the Lord. All of us are called to be a people.

We have not yet really internalised, however, that the person is the Sacrament. Despite all the good theology that has come about recently and all the hard work, there still is a very real inclination

14

within the Church community to look on the Sacraments as something done to us and of which we are passive recipients. Yes, we know we have to accept them and we have to have a vibrant faith for the Sacrament to be meaningful and to take full effect. But we don't see ourselves as active participants in the very creation of the Sacrament. We still tend to look on the Sacraments as only rituals, as actions performed by the Church as an institution. We don't see the Sacraments as persons of the Church interacting upon one another; as calls to establish a love bond between us; as calls from our family to love that family in a very special way. The net result, despite all the beautiful words to the contrary, is that we still see the Church as a *thing* rather than *us*.

As long as the Sacraments remain something that are done to us as individuals, as long as we look on these experiences as private ones for our basic spiritual self-improvement, then we're never going to see the reality of the Church and that's especially true in regard to the Sacrament of Matrimony. For Matrimony is a sign of the Church.

Much of what is said in this book is going to be about Matrimony because you can't talk about the Church without talking about Matrimony. Also, you can't talk about Matrimony without talking about the Church. The reality is that we almost never connect the two at all. At best we make some references to Church when we talk about the Sacrament of Matrimony, but we don't see Matrimony as an essential dimension to a true understanding of Church. Consequently, we feel perfectly free to talk about Church without any reference to Matrimony at all. The tragedy is that whole books can be written about the Church without a single word about the Sacrament of Matrimony.

A response often made to that statement is: "Well, what's surprising about that? Of course Matrimony is an *aspect* of Church living, but we can take the Church from many dimensions and perspectives and not consider it from the point of view of Matrimony". That basically is what this whole book challenges. We can't do that. The Sacrament of Matrimony is a dimension of Church experience essential to any true comprehension of the Church — and not just to those of us who are married. One cannot be either understood or experienced without the other. It would

15

simply be incredible to even consider Church without any reference to the Eucharist. So too it is equally incredible to seek to discern who we have been called to be by the Lord without looking at the model he himself established to provide the basic prophecy to our identity.

In this book we are looking at Matrimony in the *Catholic* Church and we are going to consider the Church in terms of those who call themselves Catholics. Obviously, this is a restricted use of the term. It provides very real limitations. The Church is obviously broader than those who are baptised Catholic. But there are very definite dimensions to being Catholic that provide insight, understanding and richness to any study of the Church. Moreover, the sacramentality of Matrimony is at least as highly developed if not more so in the specific faith community as in any other. So, in no way is there intended to be any elimination, implied or otherwise, of other Christians from the Church, the Body of Christ, the Community of Love. There is no exclusivity or triumphalism here. We will merely be limiting our perspective in order to seek a greater clarity.

2

I WANT TO BE ME

Before going any further, we have to face into personhood. For there is a heresy of individualism in general society and in the Church today that is anti-sacramental. Until we recognise this orientation as poison, we are never going to be able to understand any of the Sacraments, much less experience and practise them. For Sacraments are calls to relationship, not private individualistic experiences.

Unfortunately, however, relationship is not very much reverenced in the Church and even less in our society as a whole. We're living a life in which we worship at the shrine of individualism.

The individualism we are referring to is not the "John Wayne" type — the rugged individualist. That kind of person focused on finding his identity in the things he did that furthered self-accomplishment and development, rejecting support or help from anyone. Such help was looked upon as a sign of weakness. It was typified by the poem "Invictus": "I am the master of my fate, I am the captain of my soul". It made other people irrelevant to my life. It was a calling out to stand back. I want to do it myself. It led people to develop an iron-willed determination and an isolated independence. Obviously this was terribly inadequate and false because it depersonalised others and often excused running over them for the sake of accomplishing something I wanted to do.

We find multiple examples of it in our history — like the Robber Barons, and the Great Ranchers. Such a mentality is found in our own day, too, but it's more likely to be found in a multinational corporation and institutionalised in the Church, politics and educational systems, rather than in single individuals.

Today's kind of individualism, however, is of an entirely different variety. It's not rugged at all, either in the Church or in

17

society as a whole. It's very tentative and insecure; in fact it is almost downright demeaning. Instead of calling for us all to stand back, "get out of my way and let me do my thing", it's a plaintive trying to get my act together. Everyone has to wait until I do. It's a passive calling all around me to notice my fragility as a person; everyone has to be very protective of my process of discovering. Instead of self-accomplishment, it is self-discovery to which I put all my energies. Rather than standing apart from all people, I positively call on all people to stop everything and then to help me find my identity. I have no real relationship with them. Their purpose in my life is not for me to relate to them but for them to help me in my identity crisis, to help me in my interior voyage of self-discovery.

It leads to an incredible egoism. It's a perpetuating of adolescence. Such probing and self-examination is perfectly called for during that stage of development, but it seems many of us never get out of that. Oftentimes, it seems we're in perpetual self-analysis. As long as I'm not satisfied with where I discover myself to be with myself, or with others, than you have to wait.

Basically, it's the same mentality as the Robber Baron — totally acquisitive. Only the tactics have changed. In the other system, it was land or money or power or recognition that was the purpose of life. Now, the goal is how much I'm appreciated, how I feel about myself, how I see myself being fulfilled.

It leads people to develop a built-in escape mechanism for every failure and an excusing of themselves so they don't even have to try. How can I be expected to pass my exams or hold a job or get ahead in the company or do well with my children or succeed in my marriage or respond to the Church or whatever it happens to be, as long as I'm still mixed up about myself? I have to settle that first; then I'll take care of the other things.

It leads to a dependency, but this dependency is just as isolated as the previous independence was. In the previous case, the individual didn't care about others many times, as long as he was able to accomplish what he set his mind upon. So too, people become irrelevant unless they support my search for me. Whereas the previous individualism tended to exclude people and was typified by the slogan "Myself alone", the present situation is much more

18

exploitative. It's calling for everyone to put all their attention on helping me be pleased with me. Not to accomplish anything, not to create anything but simply to find my own person. Only then, which of course never comes about, could I even consider looking at you.

I decide my relationships, therefore, on my own terms insofar as they *fulfil* me. My view of my life, of my personal goals, of my Church or faith experience must be kept inviolable at all costs. As long as I can say that my independence is not being respected or my personal fulfilment is not happening, everything else can halt. Whereas, before, we could be domineering type personalities in insisting on getting our own way, now we hold out our sensitivity in our feelings to excuse why I am not responsive to you. If I don't have my act together, well then you just have to wait.

The number of books and the number of articles that fortify this mentality is incredible. The highest goal that we are having held out to us today is personal integrity — to thine ownself be true. March to your own drum. Follow your own conscience. (Even the emphasis on service today is an expression of this whole mentality — the self-orientation we are describing often expresses itself under the guise of helping others.)

Of course, when we put it down this way, it just seems absolutely unbelievable that as intelligent and really good individuals we can fall for this. But nonetheless, we've gone through at least a decade of it and we're still under the spell.

What has happened, of course, is that this is a reaction to the over-institutionalisation that we face both in Church and in society in general. The individual was lost. The personal good was sacrificed for the whole and, unfortunately, that whole was the institution, not the whole person. We rebelled against this and quite rightly so, and we said: "But this doesn't make any sense; we can't get people chopped up for the sake of a thing." But then we skipped over a step. We jumped from institution to individual person instead of seeing that between the two there were people — personal relationships on a one-to-one basis and on a community basis. While institutional values and goals and directions and the good of a bureaucratic system can't be allowed to replace persons and their needs, we also can't go to the opposite extreme and

19

assert in practice if not in theory that we're just a bunch of individual people, each of whom establishes his or her own way. of doing things for their own purposes and on their own terms. There has to be a very real sense of *other* in our approach to life. In our effort to reduce institutions and structures and bureaucracies to their true place, we threw out relationship and we have ended up with millions of personal islands.

It's very fashionable today to proclaim the statement that no man is an island. But what we reduce that truth to is that I have a relationship with other people in order to discover me. That simply is not true. What happens in those circumstances is that I never really get into relationships, that I just get a counsellor or an aide, or I organise a posse to chase the fugitive which is myself.

Rugged individualism, as nakedly individualistic as it was, at least was honest. Selfish yes, but openly so. The present personhood phase is manipulative and exploitative and even more aggressive than the previous way. In my pitiable weakness, I can make you feel guilty. I can take the focus off us and put it on me and all in terms of an identity crisis or a poor self-image — I'm not feeling up to it today. The rugged individualist was judged in terms of what he accomplished. The only product of today's individualism is "self" — it is a constant swirling around in the sink hole of self. It's as sterile as that. Even the goal of personal relationships becomes mutual self-fulfilment. We have lost Agape and made Eros supreme.

So all my energy, all my talents, all my concentration goes into a constant interior weather report. Where am I? How do I feel about myself? How do I judge I'm developing? How do I see my life as fulfilling? Are you meaningful to me? How am I growing as a person? Are you helping me to be fulfilled? Is what I am doing for you fulfilling to me? We minimise the sense of other in our life and maximise "I".

Of course we're bound to fail. The more we concentrate on where we are, the more we discover where we're not. The greater our emphasis on discovering what we have, the more heightened our consciousness is of what we haven't. We're made for others, not for ourselves, and it is by being for others that we most fulfil ourselves.

20

We're not, of course, denying the importance of self-identity and a certain basic ego strength in order to lead a fulfilling life. What we're saying here is that we're going about it the wrong way. We best discover ourselves in the reflection of love rather than in an interior search.

There can be no understanding of Church, much less of the Sacrament of Matrimony, in an environment which calls each of us to develop fully as individuals and then *subsequently* to talk about relationships. For the Church and each one of the Sacraments is an experience of relationship. Sacraments are not private individualistic experiences.

So one of the most significant questions I have to ask myself is "How does my being a member of the Church affect other Catholics?" — not just, "How does it affect me?" "How does my being a Sacrament of Baptism or of Holy Orders, or of Matrimony, or whatever, enhance the life of my fellow believers?" That is what should be most personally meaningful.

Our relationships must determine our personhood — not vice versa. It is other people who tell us who we are in the most positive and affirmative terms. It is those who love us and who are loved by us who can most reveal our identity to us; most obviously our parents and the other members of our family and then all the other love relationships, especially the marital one.

Instead of concentrating on me, I've got to start concentrating on you and us. Otherwise there is no hope for me. If it's just me that's looking at me and telling me who I am, then it's narrow and myopic and very definitely limited and restricted. There is a richness that others bring to the revelation of who I am that I could never achieve by myself.

But it's so hard; we are so self-oriented, and it's natural to be that way, especially in our day. It's canonised. In all the pop psychology books, in all the pop theology books, in so much of our teaching of our young — "You have got to find yourself". We send our kids on a wild goose chase. We tell them the most important question in life is self-identity — "Where am I going?: What will give meaning to my life?: Who am I?: What is my life all about?" It is not.

There is no way to answer those questions until we answer two

21

other questions. "To whom do I belong?" And, "Who belongs to me?" So many of our young adults say: "I don't belong to anybody and I don't want to." That's why they are lonely; that's why they're alienated. Nor is such alienation restricted to the young. All elements of the Church — religious, laity and priests, are deeply and painfully experiencing the cry of the lonely heart: "Who am I?" and "What is my life all about?" So we keep searching. Because we want to be ourselves. And as long as I am myself, I'm nobody. I only discover my true self in the eyes of someone who loves me. I can never discover myself by looking within. I have to take your revelation.

Most of us would accept the reality of that, but there are implied conditions on it — that I'll accept your revelation of who I am as long as I agree with it or as long as I feel comfortable with you or as long as tonight I happen to be open to you. I'm not really willing to commit myself to you regardless of the way I see you at a given moment. I am really not willing to let go and be that fully involved in a love relationship. I'll only go so far. That applies to us as human persons and it also applies to us as Church persons.

For even as Church persons we look on ourselves as individuals created in the image and likeness of God. We've got to recognise that that's not Biblical. Actually scripture tells us: "In the image of God he created *them,* male and female he created *them*".

There can be a very real resistance to this statement and the implications that are involved here because we're so personhood oriented and we want to make every individual person carry the same charisms and have the same equal dignity and worth. Yet each of us reveals the dimensions of God's world in different ways and it is specifically in terms of the relationship between male and female that God is best revealed, because God is relationship.

Consequently the individual person by him or herself is not the best image of God, because God is not an individual person. God is *persons* in relationship. So that passage in Genesis is very, very significant and carries a wealth of meaning for us all. And it's specifically in our ordination to relationship with one another in the Sacrament of Matrimony that we most image God. That is the ultimate and most complete male-female relationship. Our highest dignity is the fact that we mirror God, that we are the highest form of creation in this world and we are made in his image and likeness. But we are not made in his image and likeness as isolated individuals.

Just the very terms, male and female, to start with, are relationship terms. I'm not a male by myself. We simply cannot define male or femaleness without reference to the other sex — which is exactly why that whole reality is such a beautiful imaging of God. I cannot define God the Father without reference to the Son. His very nature is relationship. So, the very nature of man is relationship to woman. Scripture very definitely connects them in terms of our very imaging of Almighty God. So just from the point of view of our faith, we've got to start to recognise that this terrible concentration on individual personhood is poison.

When we talk about Sacraments, we have to consider them as signs. But again, signs are only effective *in terms of relationship*. Signs don't work unless there are others. So when I look at the Sacrament in terms of what I'm getting out of it and what it means to me and how it affects my life, then I'm really missing the whole point. This, of course, goes back to the fallacy that a Sacrament is something done to me rather than that I am a Sacrament who am FOR the people of the Church.

So consequently, instead of saying, "What does it do for me?", I have to be asking myself, "Who do I want to be for these fellow believers of mine?" "What do I want to be saying by who I am in the midst of this community?" "How do I want to reveal the presence of the Lord in their midst?" "How am I responding to their call?"

And it is their call, not mine. I don't establish what the message of the sign is. That has been determined by the Lord. So I have to face two things. Firstly, I have to ask myself what I am communicating to my brothers and sisters in the faith by becoming this sign, this Sacrament. Secondly, I have to face into the fact that *they* are calling me to be this sign — it is not I who have determined that I should be a sign, nor have I determined what that sign is. So am I willing to respond to them and *on their terms?* That is very significant.

For example, I might believe that the word "light" means something that is bitter and distasteful. But that is a distortion of meaning if I'm speaking English. I don't communicate anything that way because people understand it completely differently. So too with the Sacraments. Sacraments are the language of the Church, so I have to take the community's definition of what the Sacrament means and not just establish my own.

There has to be a sense of peoplehood, however, to have a common language. Unless people are in communication with one another on a regular basis, they're not going to develop a language for use among themselves. Language, after all, is meant to communicate. It's meant to build communities. Unless there's a common desire among a group of people to be a community, then no common language develops. That's one of the difficulties of the Church today. Because we're not a community, we don't have a common language. And signs only communicate to others when we speak a common language or at least understand common symbols.

We don't want to hear any call from the community. It is easier to concentrate on personal perfection and the faith of the individual person as the fundamental pre-disposition for sacramental experience. In reality, a much more important pre-disposition is our relationship with the believing community. Not just with the Lord privately, but with the Lord in the context of his people. Where we are with the Church — that is our fellow Catholics — is a more important question to ask than, "How do I feel about this particular Sacrament?"

For the Sacraments are not a disembodied gift from the Lord. They are calls to relationship with my fellow Catholics. They are the language of my family, and if I'm going to speak that language it's for the sake of being in communication with this family and not just for the sake of having the capability of speaking another language just for my own individual self-advancement and perfection. Sacraments are in, of, and for the Church, this believing community. They are established specifically in order to enable us to build a deeper sense of communion with one another in the Church.

So often we look on Jesus as disembodied. We do not see accepting the Sacraments as also accepting the people of the

24

Sacraments. We want to accept the body and blood of Jesus apart from the Body of Jesus, the Church. We don't accept the community of love that he has established. We really look on the Church as a spiritual welfare agency, so it's as if we went to a welfare office or a social security office and picked up our benefits, but we don't feel any particular ties to the people who sign our cheques or actually hand them to us. We do not see that by the very acceptance of the Sacraments we're saying we belong to you, these specific believing people.

One of the things our liturgists are complaining about is that there are no, or very few significant symbols in the Church today. They are saying you can't have a meaningful Church community without external symbols that remind us of who we are. And the reason we don't have those symbols is because we don't have a community with one another. We have made the Church a service organisation concentrating on ministry rather than on being familied with one another. We concentrate on personal development. My faith is my faith. If it happens to be similar to what you're experiencing, then fine. I'll go along with you. So I don't have any particular need for symbols. I don't see any particular call to signal to you or let others know to whom I belong and who belongs to me, because I just belong to myself.

Or, at best, I belong to a disembodied Lord. So, if I do adopt a symbol it's aimed at identifying me. It's aimed at proclaiming who I am. It's not particularly concerned with communication at all. It's not a call to you to respond to me; it's a call to you to recognise me.

It's just like the whole tendency to wear a cross instead of a crucifix; it's less identifying that way; it's less personal. What I have to ask myself really is, "Why am I wearing either one — for me to state my personal belief or for me to proclaim that I belong to a specific believing people?" Normally, the simple fact is that we don't want to be identified with anybody. All we want to do is be ourselves.

For the most part, though, we've abandoned symbols. We would much rather be anonymous and private, keeping our thoughts and our beliefs to ourselves, revealing them only to those whom we personally choose and select on the basis of our trust or our attraction to them. So I never have to reveal myself except on my terms and what I consider to be suitable and worthwhile. We've developed a catacomb mentality, except this time the defensiveness is not toward the outside world; it's toward one another. We have a personal little burrow of self and outside of that burrow we melt into the crowd. We don't want to be known.

This, of course, comes from the whole mentality of individualism that is so sanctified today. Because we don't lead a life that is relationship-oriented, naturally we're not going to assume external signs that will reveal any particular relationship with others. The Sacraments themselves become merely rituals that are done to me or Christ experiences of my own.

And if I have no experience of sacramental relationship, then my approach to Sacrament is going to be in terms of what it does for me, what it means to me, how comfortable I am with it. That will be what makes it meaningful. So I can say to myself if I don't find any personal meaning in something sacramental, that therefore it's irrelevant, it doesn't mean anything to me and I'm a phoney if I get myself involved in it.

On the other hand, if I recognise that I have a responsibility to others, that I have a call to be beyond myself, not just to take everything on my terms, but also be be responsive to my faith family and to find meaningful what they find meaningful, then my whole life will be enriched. The whole Church experience in fact is exactly that. That I'm more myself, I'm enriched, I'm enhanced, I'm expanded, that I'm not just me but I'm an expression of us. The prime purpose of sacramental experience is to open my eyes to the love that I am experiencing in the Church and to open myself to a deeper relationship with those faithful people.

Out of that deeper relationship with my fellow believers come very real responsibilities to fulfil the needs of others, to have compassion on the poor and the suffering, etc. It's a responsibility, not in myself, however, but as a member of this believing community. So I'm not reaching out as an individual: I'm speaking the whole family. It's the family that sends me to care for these people.

The basic question we have to ask ourselves in any reception of the Sacraments is, "Is it making me more familied? Am I more Church? Am I closer to these people?" Not just the people in general, but to the people of the Church. So, am I receptive to my fellow Catholics? Am I willing to let myself be influenced by them, or do I treat them the way I treat anybody else? I can't just let them have an impact on me when I approve of them and just ignore them when I don't approve of them. That's the whole point; we have to be a family with our fellow Catholics. That's the point of our sacramental life as Catholics. Not simply, "Am I a better person? Am I kinder? Am I more prayerful? Am I more generous? Am I more self-sacrificing? Do I have a greater passion for justice? All of these are wonderful and beautiful but by themselves they are not enough. They have to be an expression of my relationship with my people. They can't replace that.

It's like the difference between the question "Why do you want to get married?" and "Why do you want to commit yourself to loving this woman?" The first question is a general type of thing. Or when we really get right down to it, it's facing into what I'm going to get out of it. What's in it for me. Whereas the second question is person-oriented and other-oriented. So the same thing is true as far as marrying into the community of the Church. The basic question I have to ask myself is not "How good a believer am I?" but, "How good am I with my fellow believers?" "How much do I really love my fellow Catholics and how much do I allow them to love me and be part of my life?"

So it can't be how the Church fits into my life, or whether it lives up to my expectations, but whether I live up to these people's expectations, whether I'm fitting myself into their life. Not "Are they the kind of brother and sister that I would like to have?" but, "Am I the kind of sister or brother that enhances their lives?" "Can they count on me to speak of them wherever I am?" "Can they depend upon me to have their values and their norms?" "Is my relationship with the people of the Church evident to all who see me?" "Am I really trying to be more family with them?"

Unfortunately, however, we take our Sacraments and we separate them. We make them entities unto themselves. At best, we make them a meeting with Jesus, but we take the people away from them. We see the Church as an accidental intermediary.

It's like a wife who accepts a beautiful present from her husband, let's say a diamong ring, or a new car, and she's so delighted

27

with the gift that she forgets the giver. The significant thing about the diamond ring or the car is not it in itself; the significant thing is the husband and his love for her that he would grace her with such a magnificent present. The same thing is true with Baptism. It is a gift of the Church — the Body of Christ. Therefore, we are called to respond to that Church.

We have a perfect right to choose what faith community we accept this gift from. Just like a woman has a perfect right to choose Tom, Dick or Harry to be her husband, but once she's chosen him, then she has to be faithful to him. She just can't say, a diamond is a diamond. So we just can't say Baptism is Baptism. That's not how it came to us. We have to recognise the realities, the flesh realities. The relationships we accept and establish determine how we value the gift.

We often have much more loyalty to the institution of the Catholic Church than we do to Catholics. But loyalty has to be person-oriented. The Lord is calling us to this specific believing community, not the bureaucracy, not the rules and regulations, not the spiritual events, but these people. Our problem, because of our individualism, is that we want to pick and choose. Jesus has chosen. He has chosen US to be part of their love. Isn't that a much better way to be a Catholic? It's a call to be family.

The beautiful thing about relationship rather than isolated personhood is that I don't have to have my act together, that I don't have to have it really made. I can say I am not ready, but someone who loves me says he or she is. Love calls me beyond where I see myself. If I just count on myself for strength, for direction or faith, I'm frequently going to fail, I'm going to see what I'm missing rather than what I have. But when I'm in a family situation and I'm close and responsive, then I'm going to do a lot of things that will end up having me say, "I didn't know I had it in me". We simply have to break the chains of this selfish orientation toward me.

3

THE CALL TO BE A SACRAMENTAL FAMILY

We have just seen that the Church is a call to a love relationship with the faithful, not to individual perfection or an isolated salvation. We are called to allow our fellow Catholics to influence us, to become part of our way of thinking and our way of being. It's really pride to cut ourselves off from our brothers and sisters in the faith and just deal with them as a separate entity. Or to pick and choose those that I approve of and that I will give my trust to. The Lord has trusted them as the body of his Son. That should be sufficient for me.

That is what Baptism is all about. We are submerged, immersed, die to ourselves and then rise to a new life. We live no longer for ourselves, but for him, in his community of love, this Church of the faithful, this believing people. However, Baptism is a continuing process. It is not over and done with. We have to live it out. It would be better to say that we have to live *us* out rather than *it* out. Because Baptism is a call to us the Church.

We are so act-oriented. We so concentrate on doing the right thing that we look on Baptism as a call to spiritual chores we have to perform, to rules we have to live up to, to accomplishments we have to achieve or at best to a gnostic Jesus. That misses the whole point. Baptism is a call to relationship. All those other things are merely ways to express the relationship we have been called to with Christ incarnate in the Church.

Baptism is not a fact that has been accomplished once and for all with long-term consequences. It is a continuing process of immersion, no longer in water, but in a people. It calls us to belong to this family that the Lord has gathered during this age.

The acceptance of Baptism, therefore, cannot simply be in terms of an ever-deepening realisation of what Jesus has done to me. It has to be a continually increasing awareness of who his people are to me and who I am allowing myself to be to them.

There's a whole history of personal relationships involved with my Baptism, and for that matter with any other Sacrament. It isn't the ritual of Baptism alone that makes me Catholic. I wouldn't even know I was baptised if my mother or father didn't tell me. Not only did they tell me that I was baptised, but they told me I was baptised as a Catholic. Both messages are significant. They chose not only the reality of the Sacrament, but in a specific faith community and by that very fact, they were introducing me to that faith community and calling me to a life-long relationship with those people.

So, first of all, they had to tell me. They had to reveal the actuality. But it had to be beyond that. I mean, it could have been a solemn high baptism with 17 Bishops and it could be written in gold letters at St. Peter's so anybody who read it would say: "Boy, he was really baptised". But the fact of my baptism, if it occurred during my infancy, doesn't take until it is proclaimed to me by someone I can listen to — somebody who loves me and whom I love, someone who is in relationship with me. It's only in that circumstance that it means anything to me.

So my parents have to show me that it is important to them that I accept what they have done for me. Otherwise, it's just going to be something they did for me in the past like take me to a circus or bring me on a trip, or provide me with an education. All those are nice and have a certain impact on my present life, but none of them call me to an existing relationship. What my parents have to get across to me is that there's an existing relationship that I have to face into.

Now, obviously, that's not something I can do by myself. It's under their leadership and direction that I even consider it and it's because of their love for me and because of my experience of being tenderly cared for by them that I can even listen to something like this. For the Gospel message can never be preached objectively. No matter how persuasive the presentation may be, it's always got to be clothed in love, and love is relationship. What they do is say, "Because we love you, because we have this relationship with you, we want you to have this special faith relationship with these other people whom we love. You are so important to us that we want this faithful people to be equally important to you." In other words, it's like saying that we want our friends to be part of the resource of the whole family. We want the whole family to look on them equally as friends.

Parents also give us a sense of the reality that Baptism gives us a name, not just Charles or Nancy, but Catholic. A name gives us an identity. Our parents give us their name. So I'm a Gallagher, or a Santucci, or a Gomez, or Palowski. That tells me to what family I belong. Names are very important to people. I can't just be a nameless person. That means I don't belong to anybody. Once I don't belong to anybody then, of course, I can't even find myself. So by baptising me in the Catholic Church, my parents were making me a family member. They were calling me to a relationship with these people.

That name Catholic is a last name — not a first name. A first name is a name that distinguishes me from all other members of the same family. A last name is one that identifies me with all members of the family. Catholic is a last name. It calls me to a permanent, unbreakable relationship with my fellow Catholics in Christ.

The Sacrament of Baptism happens because we as Church believe in the Sacrament of that child's parents. It is as if we said to that mother and father: "We believe that you are faithful people. We will baptise the child even though the child doesn't know anything about what's happening and will not for a long time. But we will baptise your child because we believe that you are committed to us, and you believe in us so much that we are confident that we as Church will be present to that child in your home".

We always had assumed in the past that as long as somebody wanted their child to be baptised, that was enough of a commitment to believe that the child would be raised in the faith. We're recognising now that that, unfortunately, in some cases, is a false assumption. We're starting to say "Wait a minute, we just can't baptise anybody. We have to have some kind of assurance that it's not just a ritual being done. We have to be convinced that this

31

child will grow to know and love us and belong to us over the years". Otherwise, we would not baptise a child.

Once we have been baptised in childhood, of course, we have to ratify that decision of our parents at a later stage. We come to realise that we have been chosen and accept that choice. Now it's a personal choice. Until then it was somebody else's decision. But we can't live off the faith of our parents all our life long. We have to grow into a faith of our own and a very real personal commitment.

But it is never an individual, isolated thing. I can have a private relationship with God, but I can't be a Catholic privately. I can't be accepting these precious gifts of this believing people and ignore those people. I can't be just saying that these nice Sacraments of your I'm perfectly willing to share in, but I'm not willing to share your life. In a very real way, it's like a man who goes out with a woman for years and years, enjoys her companionship, delights in the meals that she cooks for him and is very pleased that she's always available whenever he needs a companion — but he never marries her. And an awful lot of times, that's the way that we act with the Catholic Church. We take everything the Church has to offer, but never commit ourselves to those people.

No one is saying, of course, that I have to choose to be Catholic, but what we are saying is that we can't say we're Catholic and then establish our own parameters of what Catholic is. It's a call to relationship with our fellow Catholics, not just to doing Catholic things or agreeing with Catholic principles. It's to have a unique and special love relationship with our fellow Catholics. So being Catholic can never be *my* thing, it is always *our* thing. It has to be a commitment to a way of life. It has to be an openness to live as Catholic; to accept that that's my last name; that it's not just something that I do, but it's who I am because you have made me that way. There's a very definite personal choice involved. No one forces me to be Catholic. I decide. But I don't decide what that means. We the community decide.

For being a Catholic is a call to identify myself with Catholics. Not in a restrictive way. Not in a way that rejects others, but, just like with my own family, I identify myself as this man's son. That's not putting down any other man, nor is it denying that I

32

have responsibilities to that other man if he's in need. When I say I have a blood sister, that doesn't say anything negative about any other woman or make her less, but it does positively affirm my belonging to my sister.

What it's really saying is that I'm more than myself alone. I come to you with all sorts of loves that have made me who I am. And they, these brothers and sisters of mine in the faith, are part of the love that I give to you, so it's not my own individual love alone which you have touched. There's something beautiful about that, isn't there?

The Eucharist too is a call to family. It is not just saying, "Do you believe that this isn't bread, that this is my Body?" It is also a call: "Do you believe that this isn't just a gang of people, but this is my people, my Body?" For receiving the Eucharist does not bring us to a relationship with an isolated Jesus but with a bodied one.

So often we take the Eucharist apart from the people, but I just can't go to Communion as if I were standing in line in a super-market and the people around me are irrelevant. Eating his body and drinking his blood is intended to body us more with him in his people. It is not simply for our personal spiritual nourishment. It is to build up the love and tenderness and devotion that we have for one another in the Church. The way I am fed into unity with Christ is by being empowered to be more one with his Body, the people of the Church.

"It is an essential truth, not only of doctrine but also of life, that the Eucharist builds the Church, building it as the authentic community of the People of God, as the assembly of the faithful, bearing the same mark of unity that was shared by the Apostles and the first disciples of the Lord" (Pope John Paul II, *Redemptor Hominis,* IV, 20).

Actually, the Eucharist is a Sacrament of community and its prime effect should be to help us become more involved with our fellow Catholics. It's just like a family meal. The purpose of the family meal is not just to nourish the members of the family and make them healthier or enable them to accomplish their private goals; the real purpose of the meal for a family is to make them more of a family. Eating is merely the occasion for them to concentrate on one another, to focus in on their awareness of and responsiveness to each member of the family.

So the real question is: "Does your faith centre around what you believe or the people in whom you believe? Is your faith in a beheaded Jesus, or do you believe in us, his Body? Do you recognise that you are called to a special intimacy with those who eat his Body and drink his Blood with you?"

You know, in a very real way, we act in the Church the way a husband and wife act toward one another with sex. Just like sex can be private rather than intimate. So too, our reception of the Sacraments can be the same way. The most intimate thing that we can do as Catholics is to receive the Eucharist. It should lead to a tremendous awareness of our fellow believers and a much deeper involvement in their lives. Very frequently, it doesn't at all. We just receive the Eucharist and everybody else in the Church receives the Eucharist and there are no particular increased ties to those fellow believers. We're just doing a very intimate thing with them, but we're doing it privately. It's almost as if they weren't present.

In any family, of course, there are failures. We're human beings and we're sinners. We do become selfish. We do forget our relationship with one another. We have to come to ourselves and start again. That is why we have the Sacrament of Reconciliation, to make us aware of our need to repent in the presence of our people. It isn't just in human terms that we have to express outwardly an interior change of heart. Just to make the interior change more meaningful and more purposeful to ourselves alone. If we go in the secrecy of our room and speak to our Father, it's not enough. The forgiveness in our relationship with God can easily take place privately, but the reconciliation with one another has got to be externalised.

It's just like a husband and wife. A husband can say to himself: "Gosh, I was pretty nasty to her and I won't do that any more", but he has got to tell her. So in our faith family, It's not just good enough for you to say to yourself: "Well, now I'm a different person". Tell *me* you are, tell all of us. What you tell us is not how bad you are but what you tell us is how much we mean to you and how much you want to be part of us once again.

However, that isn't the main reason we have the Sacrament of Reconciliation. We have the Sacrament of Reconciliation because we have to say: "I don't belong to you any more; I have denied you. I am no longer worthy to be called a Catholic". In other words, sin is not just a bad action; it's a breach of relationship; it's a breaking of us. The Sacrament of Reconciliation exists to face us into our relationship with Jesus in this community. For true reconciliation happens between people. It's not simply recognising I have done something bad, or even that I've hurt you. It's that I've hurt us, I've made us less.

A true coming to myself is a recognition not of what I have done, but of who I am. And who I am is never private, it's never alone, it's always a person in relationship. So for example, a husband in coming to himself recognises who his wife is and who he is called to be to her. That's when real reconciliation in a marriage takes place. So too for a Catholic. It isn't good enough to recognise that I haven't conducted myself in a proper way. It's that I'm not being responsible to my people, that I have let them down, that I have interfered with our communion with one another.

That's very difficult for us to face. We tend to accept that we are sinners and that our sins mean we fail to live up to our potential or to what Jesus has done for us, or to whom Jesus is to us, or to the level of grace that we have. But that's all self-oriented. What we've got to recognise is that we've let our family down. And more than that, we've cut ourselves off from our family. There is an infidelity involved in sin. Not just an infidelity to some ideal, or to some principle, or to a commandment, much less to our personal integrity, but to these people. We haven't lived their way of life when we've sinned. We've chosen our own way of life as more attractive.

That's when the real repentance comes in; when I don't just go to confession because it gives me a greater interior security that I have been forgiven, or even because Jesus offers it to us, or because it's been a habit since my childhood, but because we need to re-establish the relationship with our people.

In the early days of the Church, confession was public. Three particular sins they concentrated on — apostasy, adultery and

35

murder — were all sins that obviously affected the community. The first one was a flat-out denial of my relationship with the community, but the other two destroyed the reputation of the community in the ancient world in a very severe way.

We think apostasy is something we don't practise today. But we're denying our Catholic brothers and sisters constantly. We're reluctant to admit that we're Catholic a lot of times. We don't want to be tagged with them. On some issue like abortion, someone says: "Well, you only hold that because you're a Catholic," and we immediately try to prove that that has nothing to do with it. What we're really doing is we're putting them out of our life. We want to live our own life. Or we say: "No . . . No . . . I say it because I really believe it". Isn't that very interesting? If I say it because my fellow Catholics say it, the implication is that I don't really believe it. But, if I hold it on my own then it has a validity. Which is just another example of how individual oriented and how anti-relationship we are. What I'm doing is denying you. I want to stand on my own and hold my own opinion. The fact that the Church — my people — holds it too is a disadvantage.

When people can say: "Of course he says that because he's a Catholic", that means that I've allowed you to influence me, that I'm part of you and when you speak I speak, that we're a family. And that's a sign. In fact, unless people recognise you and me, unless they see your influence upon me as Church, unless it's very evident to others what faith-community I belong to, then I'm either not part of you or I'm deliberately suppressing you. There is no way of life involved, there is no sign, if being a part of this pilgrim people is just for Mass on Sunday.

There are so many other ways in which we apostasise today. Like when we live the same way as anybody else of our socio-economic class and we don't take Church values and live them out. We're denying who we are. The torture that we face today, of course, is not fire or sword; it's being considered by our co-workers or our neighbours as not being independent. And the point is not how many other Catholics are doing it. Failings of one member of the family don't excuse failings of another.

But our sins are not bad actions. They're breaches of relationship. They're the old cry of Lucifer: "I will not serve". They are the story of the Prodigal Son who wants to take his inheritance and go away from our family. And maybe we don't live riotously but the basic sin of the son was not the riotous living — it was going away from his family and denying his father. The riotous living was merely a natural consequence of wanting to be separate. So the most significant thing we say in confession is not, "I did that". It's "I don't belong to you anymore. I have put myself apart from you. I have made you, my family, less in the eyes of others. I have embarrassed you. I am not worthy to belong to the Body of Christ. I am not worthy to be a Catholic". And then, our people, the Church says: "Rejoice; my brother and my sister Catholic was lost and is now found, and they have come to life again in our midst".

So we're not focusing on what we have done but on who our people are, how wonderful and how good and how well they deserve of us. Not on how bad we've been or how miserable we are, but on the goodness of our people, the community of love that Jesus has established. In other words, we get the concentration off ourselves and on to our people.

Unfortunately, this hasn't been our training with the Sacrament of Reconciliation. We haven't been educated into looking at the goodness of our people and how absolutely open-handed is the forgiveness that our family offers us. Our training has been in self-evaluation and examination. Not in terms of a relationship with our people, but strictly in terms of what my obligations are, my responsibilities. Whether I see myself living up to the commandments.

Today, of course, it's even worse. It's even more private and isolationist so that I don't even have to go to the Sacrament. Because it's strictly my terms on which I examine my conscience. So, what we do is we look inside ourselves and see if I'm displeased with anything I've done or if I can't live with the way I'm conducting my life and so it's all my interpretation of what Jesus wants of me. Consequently, we have no need within ourselves to seek forgiveness, because basically the only one I'm looking to to provide forgiveness is myself. There's no need in my life for the Sacrament of Reconciliation because I'm already reconciled to myself. It's as horrible as that.

Previously, it was legalistic and act-oriented, granted, but at least the terms were given to us by the people of the Church. Now it's just my own way of looking at things and we don't consider what we have done to the people of the Church. At best we might consider that we hurt this individual — but not that we failed in our responsibility to this group of faithful people. We don't see what that hurt or what that failure does to the whole faith family and that we need to reconcile with that faith family. We simply cut ourselves off from our faith family and we go blithely ahead satisfying ourselves.

Instead of going to the Sacrament of Reconciliation to get the slate wiped clean or to make a fresh start personally, we need to go to the Sacrament to reconcile. Reconciliation — just the word itself — brings out much more clearly than the word forgiveness does, the personal relationship dimension. We go to confession to reaffirm our belonging to this people, to be welcomed back home, to affirm our people and our relationship with them once again. We are healed there of the scars of selfishness and born anew into relationship with God's community of love, the Church.

Our basic call, then, is to a specific, special relationship, within the people of God, with other Catholics, immersing ourselves in their way of life. Not merely by doing Catholic things. Not merely by holding Catholic principles. But by becoming family with that community of love we call our Church.

The fact is, however, that we can only discover ourselves as Catholics through other Catholics. Just as it's a husband that defines a wife and tells her who she is, and it's a wife who makes a man a husband. All too often in a marriage, unfortunately, a husband decides what a good husband is. A wife looks within herself and talks to other women to discover what a wife should be like. That simply is not going to be meaningful or successful. A man has to go to his wife and she is the one who tells him what a good husband for her is. A wife has to discover her wifeliness in her husband's eyes and from her husband's heart rather than from her own. So it's our fellow Catholics who make us Catholic. I cannot be Catholic by myself. There's no such thing as a married man without a wife. There's no such thing as a Catholic without other Catholics.

38

That's probably a saying that goes down hard. Sure, we'll accept the support of others and recognise that we need other people's help and so on. But at best we look on being Catholic as a "living side-by-side" type of thing. Actually, being a Catholic is to be *entwined* with one another. The Biblical example is far better; we are to be *bodied* with one another in Christ so that none of us can be well off, none of us can be healthy, none of us can be nourished and growing without the well-being of each of us. Just like I can't be a brother alone, I can't be a Catholic alone.

But the husband-wife relationship clarifies this point further. An awful lot of good husbands honestly go and do things for their wives that they really believe will please their wives. In fact, however, a husband would be much better off if he asked his wife what *she* wanted of him. So a lot of times, for example, he will take her out to an elaborate dinner and she'd really be much more pleased if he'd just sit and talk with her in the evening. It isn't that the man is a bad man. He's trying his best, but it's on his terms. It is not just that he can't be a husband by himself, but the very quality of being a husband is determined by what his wife is experiencing of him. A couple has to get their identity from one another.

Now we're not talking here about somebody giving up their personhood. What we're saying is that they discover the fullness of their personhood through relationship. It is not a question of giving up their identity. She is choosing her identity in choosing this man. He is selecting who he is by deciding on this woman. We determine our identity by our choice.

Remember St. Paul's beautiful phrase, "I live now, not I, but Christ lives in me. In him I move, I have my entire being". Okay, now substitute husband and wife there. "I live now, not I, but my wife lives in me. In her I live, I move, I find my entire being." That's what the Sacrament of Matrimony means. That's what bone of each other's bone, flesh of each other's flesh means.

In the same way, our identity has got to come from our relationship with our fellow Catholics and not from our individual activities. We are called as Catholics to belong to one another.

One of the most difficult things for us to believe psychologically is that we are the personal, individual, unique choice of Jesus. I

39

think we fall into the trap of saying, "Well, I'm a Catholic because I was born a Catholic", or "Somebody baptised me when I was a kid, and I've been going to Church all my life, so I might as well continue to do so". We don't see the personal picking out of us by him. We may, if we have a strong faith, really believe that we have a personal relationship with Jesus. But to be specifically chosen by him to belong to this people which is his Body — that's something that we have yet to internalise. That he deliberately chooses us. "From age to age he gathers a people to himself." He makes a choice to love these specific people.

That is one of the obviously outstanding qualities of marriage; they have chosen one another. Even in a society that has arranged marriages, the marriage really doesn't take place until they choose one another, until they say Amen to the choice their parents have made. And that's probably one of the most beautiful and magnificent aspects of marriage. The individual free choice. She chose this particular man to be her husband. No matter how outrageous he may be on occasion, no matter how thoughtless or frustrating, this is her special choice. He chose this woman to belong to him as his wife. She may not always live up to the ideal that he hopes for. She may be very irritating at times, but she still is his choice to belong to in a most unique way. There is no one else like her.

A woman and a man who choose one another say by that choice that their husband or wife is absolutely unique and absolutely special. They're not saying that other people are not unique and special in their own way. What they are saying is that this man or this woman is their choice. He/she is special to me, is my personal, unique choice.

The same thing is true as far as Jesus' choice of us in the Church is concerned. It is the risen Lord present in our midst who is embracing me and choosing me to be bodied with him. He has chosen me and you to be a special love of his. We look at Mary. We are awed and quite properly so at the fact that God could choose any woman to be the Mother of God. Therefore, we just wonder at Mary because she bodied the Son of God. In a very real way, each of us in the Church has been chosen to be Mary today. We have been chosen to body Jesus. It is as though the Angel of the Lord appeared to Fran or Pete or Sue and gave them glad tidings, and we have to say, "So be it, I will flesh Jesus".

We don't particularly like to face into this because when we recognise that we are chosen it seems to imply that we look on ourselves as superior. That's not true at all. He hasn't chosen us because we're better than anybody else. He's chosen us because he loves us in this specific special way. It's not saying he doesn't love other people equally. It may well be that he has chosen us to be his body for the sake of those other people that he loves. And we are a part of his expression of love to them. But the real thing that we have to recognise is that deep down what holds us back from facing into our being chosen is that it brings a sense of responsibility along with it and it calls for a response. Whereas if we can be just like anybody else, then we don't have to make any special response. So that our reluctance to face being chosen comes not out of any humility on our part but from a sense of not wanting to be that close.

We simply don't want to be that close to our fellow Catholics. We want to have our own spiritual life. We want to have our own way of doing things. We want to have our own way to respond to the Lord, and we want to fit the Lord into our life on our terms. And we don't want our life to be cluttered up with all these other people; we just want to have Jesus by ourselves. This is the whole notion of privacy again.

Really the problem doesn't centre in on "Why should Jesus choose me?" or "Why didn't he choose others?" or "Other people are equally good". We use all those arguments, but the real trouble of the matter is we simply don't want to be that identified as Catholics. We don't like the way a lot of Catholics are acting. We don't like the direction that this community is going and we want our independence and we want our freedom. So fundamentally we're rejecting the choice. We want to keep ourselves apart. We just don't like Catholics that much. And so Jesus says to me, "Be Catholic". And I say, "No, I'd rather have a relationship with you", or, "I'd rather be open to everybody", or "I'd rather relate to you as a Christian". He says, "Be Catholic": That's what I have to face into. He says to me, "Join yourself with these people. If

41

you want to have a relationship with me, then relate to me in, with and through this believing community of mine".

It's just like a man — he's not only chosen in terms of his relationship with her. He's also chosen by her in terms of his relationship to their children. She knows she's marrying not just a husband but a father of those kids and that therefore he is not facing her choice if he doesn't build up an intense relationship with those children. That's part of his relationship with her. Too many men make a real dichotomy between their marital relationship and their parental relationship. That simply doesn't wash as far as the wife is concerned. She really finds it very difficult to trust his relationship with her if he doesn't have an intense relationship with their children. She's perfectly correct in that distress. Those children are an expression of their marital relationship.

In the same way, an essential part of our relationship with Jesus is our relationship with our fellow Catholics. They are not two different relationships.

That's threatening, of course. We would much prefer to be free, to be independent. That's the word. Independent. That's exactly what defines where we are as far as our fellow Catholics are concerned and that's the basic problem. We simply don't want to be that involved with them. That's why we don't even want to consider something like choice. We want to go through life our own way making our own decisions and not having to be cluttered up with these interlocking relationships. We want to be independent of them. We don't want to be named with and by them.

It's like a husband who wants to have all the advantages of marriage and all the gifts that his wife gives him and yet he wants to identify himself as a lawyer or as a doctor primarily, rather than as a married man. He doesn't want to be too closely tied to her. He wants to be known as free and independent. And Jesus is saying, "I have chosen you. You have not chosen me". Therefore, it is he who chooses the parameters of what our relationship is going to be — and the choice that he has made is that we belong to this specific believing community, our fellow Catholics.

So how are our fellow Catholics experiencing us? For the very quality of our being Catholic is determined by what they experience of us. The truth of the matter is, however, that often they're not experiencing anything of us other than at best our physical presence once a week or possibly some few actions we perform in the parish.

It is also important to ask ourselves how other people who are not Catholic experience us. Do they simply see us as just like them? Or a very good person who happens to go to Mass on Sunday? Or do they see us in relationship with our fellow Catholics, part of a Catholic family? For I cannot recognise a husband in terms of what he does for *me* or how good a *man* he is, but in terms of his relationship with his wife. I may see a woman as a very, very good woman but I can only see her as a *wife* in terms of her relationship with her husband.

Similarly, we are continually turning the Church into an association of good people doing good things and thereby we are well taken care of by the Church through the Sacraments, and through prayer and through our association with other good people. Instead of recognising that we are above all called to love one another in the Lord.

Part of the problem of course, is that we want to love all men without distinction. That's not what Jesus did. That's a nice, attractive, democratic ideal, but it simply doesn't work. All of us pick and choose those we're going to love. I may choose to love those who are in extreme physical need and give them my priority. Or those who are ignorant or those who are lonely, or those who are affluent, or those who are personally attracted to me. But there's only one me. I can't love millions of people. I can't spend an equal amount on them one by one.

There's no question that we're called to perform a loving service for any person in need with whom we come in contact but we're called to specific close love relationships in addition to that. We recognise this in the practical sense of the term. It's silly for a man to be loving everybody in the neighbourhood and not spending any time with his wife and children. A woman can play lady bountiful all over the city, but there's something deficient in that love no matter how sincere it may be if the quality of life of her children and her husband are depressed. Everybody recognises that a husband and wife can't spend all their time and love on one

43

another, but all their love has to *start* with one another and be an expression of their love for one another.

So, if our vocation in the Lord is to be Catholic, then one of our priority relationships has got to be our fellow Catholics, not because they're in need, not because they're attractive, not because they're educated, not because they happen to agree with me, but specifically because they're Catholic. If I have a brother my relationship with him is determined just by the fact that he is my brother. I have a specific calling to act as a brother toward him. Of course, if I have £5.00 and somebody is starving and needs that money and my brother wants the £5.00 to go to the beach, then I would give the money to the person who is starving, but I have a priority love-relationship with my brother.

We simply don't want to admit that we have a special relationship with Catholics. We excuse ourselves and say that Catholics are no different from anybody else, just like my brother is no different from any 13-year-old boy or 42-year-old man. But he is to me. The difference is not that this man or this woman is any better than any other human being on the face of this earth. The difference is in my relationship with them. So it may be, for example, that I wish I had a different brother than I have, but he's still my brother. The same thing is true as far as my fellow Catholics are concerned.

"You can't do that", you may say, "It's a pluralistic society and there are so many needs around". Well, first of all, as far as my vocation from the Lord is concerned, he didn't *call* me to a pluralistic society. He didn't even *call* me to a specific nationality, he called me to be Catholic. He gathers a people to himself from generation to generation and he wants them to be a people, to very definitely have a close-knit love relationship with one another. Very unique and very special and being given priority. So much so that he made us his body. Yes, other Christians are members of his body, too and we do have a special relationship with them but we have a priority relationship with Catholics.

That isn't saying we should exclude anybody else or deny the beauty of their relationship with Jesus. But we are saying that if we deny our special relationship with our fellow Catholics then our relationship with all these other people is equally suspect. In a

44

way, it's like the husband who says that his love for his wife and his love for his friends is at the same intensity and of the same quality. This not only puts into question his love for his wife; it really challenges his love for his friends also. So if someone says he doesn't have a special love for his fellow Catholics, it's hard to believe that he has a very meaningful love for any other Christian either.

The Sacraments that we receive are not offered to us in a non-denominational way. The specific faith experience that Jesus has called us to is not a matter of indifference. But too often we act toward our fellow Catholics the way a lot of husbands and wives act toward one another. They set up each of them their own definition of what marriage is and make the other person fit into that. So in effect they're making a marriage of two singles. So too, when we do this in the Church we're turning the Church into an association of individuals rather than an intimate close-linked family with special ties to one another.

Even with respect to the tremendous needs that are around, we have a responsibility for those, but it is a responsibility as a member of the family, not as individuals, so we have to respond as a whole Church and in the name of the whole Church and not just as private persons. It isn't that we're supposed to do all he instructed us to do in Scripture just promiscuously across the world, but we're to do them primarily within the Catholic faith community and then exploding out of that community. The community spreads across the world and serves the world. We are not called as individuals to establish his kingdom; it is the Church that is called to do that. The more we do as individuals, the less we accomplish. The more we create a family sense among our fellow faith believers, the more his kingdom will be served.

4

THE COUPLE AS PROPHET

Now this is where Matrimony comes in as a sign. Matrimony is the prime Sacrament *of* Church. We're not saying Matrimony is *the* prime Sacrament. We would obviously say the Eucharist is the prime Sacrament, or better, that the Church itself is the prime Sacrament. What we're saying though is that Matrimony is the Sacrament that most reveals the Church itself. Therefore, it is the prime Sacrament *of* Church. It's particular charism is to reveal who the Church (we the people) is — the beloved of Jesus.

The term "bridegroom" was applied by Jesus to himself. The Church itself considered itself to be his bride. (Notice, it's the Church as community — not individual members of the Church.) Her understanding of her relationship with Jesus was very definitely in a matrimonial context. So it is our sacramental couples who can teach us what a basic love community is, how to establish it and lead the way toward it's accomplishment.

Jesus, of course, is a sign of contradiction to the world. Much that the world looks on as horrors or evils, the Lord provides a totally different light upon, such as the poor or humility. Marriage very definitely falls into this category. The traditional attitude to marriage in this world is one of cynicism and suspicion; a figure of fun with all sorts of jokes about men, about women, about marriage. Jesus comes and takes this human relationship that is so flawed, scorned and laughed about, and makes it the key way to reveal how he is speaking to us and dealing with us.

As Catholics today we really have a very poor self image. We need to find our identity as being loved by Jesus in the Church. And it is through our couples' love for one another that we can even hope to believe that. A couple is called to reveal how Jesus loves the Church — to find delight in one another; to really enjoy one another; to be continually, daily choosing one another; to be intimate; to be faithful to one another; to be two in one flesh; to find their very identity in one another.

Man in Matrimony is called to love his wife as he loves his very body — in other words, as Jesus loves the Church. When our sacramental couples are stretching to love to this degree, there is hope that we can believe that we as Church are the body of Jesus. We find that so difficult — even to grasp the idea, much less to make it our own. That we are bone of Jesus' bone, flesh of his flesh. We need the witness of the Sacrament of Matrimony, our faithful couples loving each other to that degree, with that completeness, to begin to accept that Jesus is so much involved with us in the Church. It is the very love-relationship of the couple that we are called to take as the model of our relationship to one another, the kind of community of life that we are called to as Catholics; they speak who the Church is to be to one another.

That word "who" has been very carefully chosen. The real question has to be: "Who does it mean to be a Catholic?" and it means to be a lover of my fellow Catholics and through that love to be a lover of all mankind. Just like for a husband and wife it's not "what is a husband?" — it's "who is a husband?" It's one who is the lover and beloved of his wife, and in a sacramental marriage, in that very love for her and her returned love for him, belonging to us the Church.

All the Sacraments actually are calls to relationship with the community of love, the Church, but this is one in which there is a tri-partite relationship. There is a man and a woman and the community of believers and it's the man and woman in relationship with one another and with the rest of us that is the Sacrament. It is the community of life they establish not only with one another, but with us that is their vocation in life. Without us they are not a Sacrament. Sacraments are Church experiences.

The question often asked of engaged couples is "Why do you want to get married *in* the Catholic Church?" not, "Why do you want to get married *at* the Catholic Church?" Another way of asking the same question is: "Why do you want to be a sign of who we are — namely, the beloved of Jesus? Why do you want

47

to identify Catholics to themselves by the way you love this man or woman?" Because that is what sacramental marriage is. In a very real way, the preposition should be, "Why do you want to get married *into* the Catholic Church?" Not just *in* it.

Unfortunately, however, the Church involvement of the Sacrament of Matrimony has not been very well explained or understood. The involvement of the believing people in the couple's love-relationship with one another has been pretty much limited to the wedding day with some sexual ethics thrown in. This is a tremendous loss. Not least for the couple themselves, because what's really happening is that they're being pushed into just making it on their own. They have no consciousness or a very minimal consciousness that the Sacrament of Matrimony is not just between the two of them, but is a Church experience. It's sad that, up until this time, the teaching Church has pretty much concentrated on making sure that the ceremony is done right and the couple does well with one another. There has been no real catechesis of what the couple is to do for us; what their role is among us and how they minister to us.

The wedding ceremony, of course, is very important to the couple involved. But it's even more important to the faithful. The wedding ceremony is a sign and a symbol to all of us in the Church that this couple has a new vocation in our midst. The wedding is not a little celebration that an affectionate parent throws for the children; it is an ordination ceremony.

The ceremony is also very, very important as a catechesis of what their sacramentality is. It's to remind them "Listen, this isn't just the two of you. We're just as much involved as you are. You have to remember us and you have to make us part of your love". So the wedding ceremony proclaims to the couple, first and foremost, but then to the rest of the Church: "This is a living, breathing Sacrament! Treat them with reverence. Listen to them faithfully. They have been chosen from our midst to be prophets to the reality of who we are as a people". It's a call to our brothers and sisters in the faith to look at and to respond to this man and woman differently. Now they are no longer two. We are called to listen to them as they establish their coupleness. To learn the way of life that we are to establish with one another as Church. At the wedding ceremony, it is publicly proclaimed that they have a new mission to us.

The wedding ceremony is not the Sacrament of Matrimony in itself. It's an announcement of that Sacrament. It publicly proclaims that they are not just married but matrimonied. They are not just a couple but *our* couple. Their way of life is not private but an experience of and for the whole Church. It should very definitely establish in the minds of the faithful and in the minds of the couple that it's not the couple but the Church that calls them to be a Sacrament in our midst.

So their sacramentality doesn't come from how much they love one another or how well they do with one another. That's beautiful, good and wonderful, but that's marriage. Matrimony comes from the inter-relationship that they as a couple are called to with *us,* so the sacramentality does not depend upon individual holiness or prayerfulness. It doesn't depend upon how magnificently each one of them fulfills their function as husband or wife, but it is who they are willing to be as a couple to us that makes them a Sacrament.

Furthermore, it is we the Church that makes the call, so in a very real way they're taking their vows to us as well as to one another. As a matter of fact they do not ask the question of one another and they do not establish the circumstances in which the questions are asked. It's the community of believers that does both.

The sad fact of the matter is, however, that our couples have been stuck with baptismal spirituality. Not that that's bad in itself but they are not two individuals any more. They are one love. And this is terribly important for us in the Church today, because our notion of community is so flawed and our whole experience of responding to others rather than to self to find our fulfilment, has been so weakened, that we really need to listen to the prophets in our midst — our matrimonied couples. They can't just determine what is good for them as an individual isolated man and woman any more. They have to determine everything now from a double relationship point of view. How does it make them more a couple and how does it make them more belong to us — they have to continually ask themselves what we the Church are experiencing of their relationship.

For the living out of Matrimony is just as much a Church experience as any Liturgy, as any Sacrament; therefore the couple has very definitely to be conscious of the Church in their choices to love. Matrimony is a Liturgy. The lived-out love that the couple experience with one another is a liturgical event daily celebrated, minute by minute. How our matrimonied couples express that Liturgy is as vital to us as how the individual priest celebrates the Eucharist.

Now the Sacrament of Matrimony is not something that is injected into a couple. It does not come from outside. The Sacrament of Matrimony is the faithful couple itself, living out and experiencing the mystery that is us as Church. It's the love that they experience with one another that is their Sacrament. The Sacrament is the daily way of life that they establish with, in and for one another *in the Church*. It is not a supernatural bank account of supernatural gifts.

An awful lot of times, we taught Matrimony in terms of having the graces to live your state of life. So you automatically get the implication that it's a tough hard life. And that's why the Lord had to have a big storehouse up there to take you out of trouble.

Nobody is denying the existence of grace. We're certainly not questioning the fact that there are very specific marital graces that are accorded to the sacramental couple to help them to be the sign that they are called to be. That's the point. All too often when we talk about the graces of the Sacrament of Matrimony, we talk about the problems that people are going to face in their marriage and the graces are strengths to carry crosses or to bear burdens. Or to give us patience under provocation to put up with the difficulties that we can normally expect to face in marriage and family life. Or when he's been cruel or she's been thoughtless. It's interesting that the graces of the Sacrament of Matrimony tend to focus on making up for the other person's failure. Actually they're really not the graces of the Sacrament of Matrimony at all; they are more baptismal graces than they are matrimonial ones.

The graces of the Sacrament of Matrimony are not graces to the individual person; they're to the couple and they primarily concern themselves with the couple's relationship with the overall Church. The matrimonial graces are really much more focused on who we are to the Church rather than who we are to one another. They are to be a reminder to the couple of their mission to us – so that the couple's relationship can be a proper catechesis of a faith family. Therefore, the success of the Sacrament of Matrimony is not determined by the fact that they don't get a divorce, but by how meaningfully they teach us how to belong to one another, how they love one another for our sake and how their very love for each other is at our service in the Church.

The specific graces of the Sacrament of Matrimony, then, concentrate more on the unity that they are to achieve, the prophetic role they are called to in the Church, than graces such as long-suffering, endurance, patience, self-sacrifice. These graces, of course, are important, but they're really graces all of us in the Church need. Married people don't need them any more specifically than religious or single people do. Oneness with one another and with us is the specific vocation of the Sacrament of Matrimony as established by the Lord and it is on those terms that the graces centre. More along the lines of prophecy rather than endurance. Teaching and preaching rather than control of temper. More along the lines of helping them to recognise their vocation to speak to the whole Church by the way that they love one another. Not simply to help them to get along and to avoid friction.

We certainly recognise that the Sacrament of Priesthood is for the sake of the whole Church and our concentration during the ceremony of ordination is very, very much in terms of the relationship that the priest is to establish with his people. Nor is there any question but that the individual couple profits tremendously in their own relationship because of the sacramental call. But couples have to recognise that they are ordained to the Church as much as a priest is.

They have chosen to marry one another but the Church has called them to be *matrimonied* to one another. Therefore, the Church has a very real say in what their mission is. Just as a man cannot determine what ordination means and what priesthood means – he has to go to the people of the Church and they have to reveal to him his identity as a priest. So too, with the Sacrament of Matrimony. In fact, in a very real way we can say that the Church has an even bigger stake in the Sacrament of Matrimony than it does in the Sacrament of Orders, because there are so many more matrimonial Sacraments than there are sacerdotal ones. More importantly, the Sacrament of Matrimony is specifically intended to reveal the interior identity of the Church.

What we are saying is that the Sacrament itself is this flesh and blood couple. Not just any couple, but a couple who have been chosen by the Church to be a Sacrament and who have accepted that call. They are linked together in ordinary everyday terms, livingroom, bedroom, diningroom, kitchen, at 25 Longview Terrace. That life of love is a parable of how Jesus sees us, his people. He gathers us to himself the way a husband and wife embrace one another as beloved. I don't think we in the Church see ourselves as that. I think we see ourselves as called to do a job, to live up to responsibilities. At best to love him, or at worst to be taken care of and pleased. That's not his prime calling to us. He said: "Will you be my beloved?" "Will you belong to me?" "Will you make your life with me?" "Will my people be your people?" "Wherever I go, will you go?" "Wherever I lead, will you follow?" That's the sacramental sign.

This is what a husband and wife do with one another best. They are the most meaningful expression of total belonging in human terms that we have. They really do commit themselves to a life of being each other's beloved, of belonging to one another, of making their life with each other, of going wherever the other person goes, following the other's lead, of not only living with the other person, but living as the other person lives.

The sacramental couple, moreover, has to expand beyond that. They have to look at the faith family that has called them to be a Sacrament and say: "This is my people and wherever they go I will go; wherever they live I will live". In other words, what they have to do is not only establish a community of life with one another as husband and wife, but they have to establish a community of life as a couple with this community of love, the Church. Our whole self-understanding as Church is best spoken by the way our couples love one another.

If what we experience from our sacramental couples in their

52

relationship with one another is a dull, settled-down getting-along with one another, each doing their own thing, then in those couples we are going to see our basic call as the Church. Being Catholic is not exciting, it's something we have to do. It's dull and we do our own thing without being too bad about it, without hurting each other intentionally and we settle down.

If our sacramental couples are dutiful toward one another, then that's what we will be as Church — a dutiful group of people living out responsibilities with greater or less fidelity.

If our couples are lifeless or if they carefully, oh, so carefully measure out the life they allow their love to create, then we will have a Church that is uninterested in new life. We will have a Church where missionary zeal is very low. We will have a Church where conversions are a matter of indifference or at least not very high on our list of priorities.

If we have husbands and wives who are unfaithful to one another, we will have a Church where abandonment and rejection is high.

If we have a situation in which our couples do not see that they are called to relationship beyond attraction, that their commitment to one another endures whatever their feeling at any particular time, then we will have a Church where we do not belong but merely attend or are part of when the spirit so moves us.

If we have marriages where they are living side by side, but with no real relationship, then that is the kind of Church we are going to have too.

If marriage is a power struggle between a man and a woman as to who is going to run this show, then that is what we will see in our Church. Through all the various elements of the Church, priests and laypeople, we will all be involved in: "Who's in charge here?"

If the standards of marriage are determined outside the husband and wife relationship, by what the media say or what the psychiatrists say, then the same thing is true in the Church. It is interesting that the experts on a normal love-relationship are the ones who are the professionals in dealing with those who are all messed up. And the experts on what the Church should be doing are sometimes people who are faithless or merely professional. We're not saying that they shouldn't have anything to say, nor that we should ignore their advice, but sometimes they make great sense in human terms and they miss the whole point that they themselves are not experiencing what it means to belong to us. It's just like in the husband/wife situation. Something may be perfectly right in the textbooks, but it's totally irrelevant for this couple. The basic question we have to ask of any teacher in the Church, no matter what their credentials may happen to be, is: "How much do you belong to us? How faithful are you to us? How much are you experiencing the life that we are leading?" That's something beautiful that husbands and wives teach us. A husband may have great ideas about what a wife should be like, but if he's not linked to her and part of her way of being, then what he has to say is going to be much more cold logic than it is living help.

If a couple look on marriage as a series of activities that they perform with one another then that's what our Church is going to be. Most important of all, our couples cannot allow their awareness of the relationship they have with one another to be buried in all sorts of other activities, the job, their children, the home, their social responsibility. It is just like a priest. A priest is called to do all sorts of wonderful things, and he definitely has to respond to those things, but always in the context of his priesthood. Often enough married people make their marriages a part-time affair. They have all sorts of other responsibilities and obligations which they live up to very faithfully and loyally, and they fit their marriage into those obligations. They do not see that all those obligations have to be an expression of their marriage, and fulfilled in, with, and through their love for one another.

If our couples themselves don't highlight their marriages, how is the rest of the Church going to see them? If our couples take their marriage for granted, why shouldn't we? If our couples get distracted from their marriages and fill their lives with all sorts of other things and find their meaning in life through their parenthood, in their occupation, or in the causes that they have given their hearts to, then why shouldn't we see them the same way? A man or a woman in their Sacrament of Matrimony can bury it and push to the foreground other engagements and causes so that we lose sight of the fact that they are married, and we have lost their Sacrament. Where is the witness there? Simply in the fact that they are not divorced, that they have nice children, that you never hear anything bad about them.

No, we have to make our marriage the most evident things about our life, what gives us our identity and what fulfills all the other things we do. It is time for our couples in the Church to speak up, not in opposition to anyone else, not to gain their rightful place in the sun, but to affirm who they are in the Lord, who they have been called to be by his body, the Church.

On the other hand, if our husbands and wives are love-oriented rather than accomplishment-centred, then that's the kind of Church we are going to be.

If the whole of the couple is greater than the sum of the two persons, then the whole of the Church will be greater than all of us as individuals added up. For what our couples have to bring out is that Jesus has chosen us as his Church. He has chosen personally and continuously, daily to love us with everything within him. He is absolutely indefatigable and relentless in his choosing of us and it's not a choice that's once made and lived out loyally; it's a delighted daily choice. That's the way our couples have to be with one another.

Matrimony can't be two individual people each of whom are getting an equal amount of satisfaction, fulfilment and happiness as separate individuals. It has to be as a couple, not as singles, that they live their life. That's probably the biggest lesson that they could teach us in the Church. Sometimes we can fall into the trap of saying that if everybody's happy, that's what we're aiming at. But I am called to the Church not in terms of what I as an individual get out of it, or even what I might personally contribute to having other people get out of the Church. But I am called to the Church to become an *US*. So it's we that are growing in our unity.

If the husbands and wives are focused primarily upon communication, then the Church will be more interested in communication than in being right. Making correct decisions, forming proper judgements, having the right vision of what life is all about is obviously very, very important. But as any husband and wife have experienced deeply, making being right the overall concentration in their life together can kill their love. They may be incorrect and mistaken, but the even bigger mistake would be to miss the point that their relationship with one another is their prime call. And the same thing is true in the Church. If we're responsive to our brothers and sisters, if we really listen to them and if we show them that our love for them is our prime goal in life, then they're going to be responsive to us. That's really the best way to get them to change.

Moreover, if our couples are tenderly forgiving of one another as a way of life, then that will be our experience in the Church. One of the most important qualities of Jesus' love for us in the Church is the quality of forgiveness. I think we celibates find it very difficult to forgive. I think we can be understanding. I think we can be very tolerant of other people's weaknesses. The perfect example right now is the Church's urgency for justice. That is a celibate virtue. But love has a much higher value than justice. That is one of the main reasons why we need the love dimension that only the couple brings to be dominant in the leadership of the Church and in influencing the Church's choices. I really believe that husbands and wives truly forgive one another. It doesn't always happen. In fact, it is probably fairly rare. But I believe that it happens more often in marriage than in any other human relationship. It is really possible to be at each other's throats one minute and then thirty seconds later to be in each other's arms. And I don't mean it just as a palliative but a true coming together, a real healing. Husbands and wives really do know the difference between excusing and forgiving.

The parallels between our couples and the Church as a community are simply phenomenal. It's not pious words when we say that the sacramental couple are the sign of who we see ourselves to be. And that vocation to prophesy to the Church creates a whole different way of life than mere marriage would.

This different life-style of our couples is not just a matter of: "We're Catholics, so we won't divorce one another. We'll stick by one another". Actually, that is a beautiful reality which usually is poorly explained. A couple's irrevocable choice of one another speaks Jesus' own choice of his Church. For a very comforting thing about the love Jesus has for his people, the people of the Church, is that he is never going to take it back. It is irrevocable.

He tells us in Scripture: "I will be with you all days". The choice that he makes of us is going to be there forever. He will never, ever change it. You can set up in human marriage many reasons why divorce not only should be permitted, but encouraged. I don't think you could support on a natural level that divorce is wrong. Where divorce is wrong is in the sacramental marriage, and only because it lies. It says, "Here is the way Jesus loves the Church" and he does not love us that way. He loves us exclusively with permanence. There is no intimacy compared with the intimacy with which he loves the Church. Therefore, if that intimacy is breached, if that consent in marriage is broken, then what we're saying is that that is the way Jesus loves his Church. And that is not true. If divorce were permitted in such circumstances it would make the Sacrament a false sign. (Now we're not talking about sin here and we're certainly not in any way being indifferent to the tremendous need for compassion that we should have in our hearts for our brother and sister Catholics who are separated or who are divorced. That is a moral and pastoral problem that calls for a tremendous response on the part of all of us. Here we are dealing with the sacramental dimension.)

But the uniquely different thing about our couples is not just that they choose one another irrevocably — it is that they are called to have a different type of relationship with one another in their marriage than with all others. So first of all, they are not just supposed to be two good baptised people who happen to be living together and whose spirituality is in terms of what spirituality is for the rest of the Church. Secondly, they have to recognise that they have to have a different marriage than what is being experienced in this world. Consequently, they can't just go to the gurus of this world, the psychiatrists and psychologists, the women's magazines and pop newspaper articles to discover how they are supposed to be relating to one another.

If the marriages that we are seeing in the Church are not all that much different just in human terms than the ones we see in society around us, it is going to be very difficult for the Church as a whole to see its own treasure. The vocation of the Sacrament of Matrimony is to reveal the Church to itself. To give the Church its special identity. Our identity is not of this world. So if the marriages that we see in the Church are of this world, speak of this world's values and this world's concerns, then we can well understand why the Church is so worldly. The corrective in our time, in our age, of the distortion of the Church is the Sacrament of Matrimony. It is couples loving one another in an extraordinary way and as a model of Jesus' love for the Church that will bring about the call to the real reformation of the Church and reconciliation among us.

Just as the priest has a special calling to the Sacrament of.the Eucharist, to treasure it, to revere it, and to prophesy to the presence of that Sacrament in the midst of the Church, so also our couples have a very special calling to prophesy to the Sacrament of Matrimony, and to make it so present, so vibrant and alive in the midst of the community of believers, to tell the Church that it is irresistibly attractive.

So our relationship with one another in marriage has to be visibly different. We have to look at ourselves and see what we are saying to other people by the way we are living with each other in marriage. We are not talking here about jobs or how we spend our money or lifestyle; we are talking about love-style here. If sacramental husbands treat their wives the same way as other good nonsacramental husbands, then of what meaning is the Sacrament?

We really have not accepted Matrimony as a full-fledged Sacrament. We don't see the Church dependent at all upon the Sacrament of Matrimony, other than in the matter of divorce. And so it's only from a negative point of view that we recognise that Matrimony has an impact upon the Church. We don't see the positive dimension of it at all. We really don't see our married couples in their very marriage as creative of the Church.

What we need to do is to get our eyes and attention off the problems of marriage and begin to concentrate on the potential of marriage. It seems that any time marriage is brought up, the conversation soon centres around the divorce or the difficulties we have with our children or the fights or the lack of understanding that exists. No one, of course, is trying to stick the head in the sand or to deny that these things are real issues. What we are saying is that the overriding issue of marriage is the couple and their love for one another. We are not facing into that very much

second time. Let anything left be for the stranger, the orphan and the widow.

'Remember that you were a slave in the land of Egypt. That is why I lay this charge on you.

'If men have any dispute they must go to court for the judges to decide between them; these must declare the one who is right to be in the right, the one who is wrong to be in the wrong. If the one who is in the wrong deserves a flogging, the judge shall make him lie down and have him flogged in his presence with the number of strokes proportionate to his offence. He may impose forty strokes but no more, lest the flogging be too severe and your brother be degraded in your eyes.

'You must not muzzle an ox when it is treading out the corn.'

2nd Reading: The Constitution on the Church in the Modern World (N 48)

As God of old made himself present to his people through a covenant of love and fidelity, so now the Saviour of men and the bridegroom of the Church comes into the lives of married Christians through the sacrament of matrimony. He abides with them thereafter so that, just as he loved the Church and handed himself over on her behalf, the husband and wife may love each other with perpetual fidelity, through mutual self-bestowal.

Authentic married love is caught up into divine love and is governed and enriched by Christ's redeeming power and the saving activity of the Church. Thus this love can lead the husband and wife to God with powerful effect and can aid and strengthen them in the sublime office of being a father or a mother.

For this reason, married Christians have a special sacrament by which they are fortified and receive a kind of consecration in the duties and dignity of their state. By virtue of this sacrament, as husbands and wives fulfil their conjugal and family obligations, they are penetrated with the spirit of Christ. This spirit suffuses their whole lives with faith, hope and charity. Thus they increasingly advance their own perfection, as well as their mutual sanctification, and hence contribute jointly to the glory of God.

right now. We are trying to solve the problems of the disasters of marriage instead of offering new horizons, new hopes and building on the potential.

In the training to the priesthood we don't centre around the priests who are leaving or the priests who are not living up to their opportunities. We centre around the real call of priesthood. We try to offer our young men the fullest horizons they are capable of reaching, to encourage them to be the most priest they can. But in marriage we seem to do just the opposite. We concentrate on pointing out the dangers they can fall into, how to avoid the traps. That is almost a guaranteed way to hold down the level of performance in marriage. It is almost certain to make our people look on it as a second class vocation, to make certain that our married people will not have that much respect for themselves or much ambition to accomplish greatness in their marriage. We simply do not look on Matrimony as a vocation of the Church the way we look on religious life or priesthood, and consequently, this attitude has gotten across to our people. They don't see their marriage as a prophetic voice in the Church; they don't see that they're ordained to the community of the faithful.

Really if you ask somebody what is a good marriage, it seems that the pinnacle of success is that we settle down and both parties are mutually satisfied. Well, we have got to shoot much higher than that. We have got to look at what it means to be two in one flesh. What it means to leave all things and cling to our wife. What it means for a man to love his wife as he loves his own body. For a woman to be completely responsive to her husband. What it means to love one another as Christ loves the Church.

So one of the biggest jobs we have to do within the Church is to persuade our couples that their love is not private. That their Sacrament is not something the Church does for them, but something they do for the Church, in the Church. That the intensity of their absorption in one another is one of the greatest graces God has given the Church to spend upon the world.

What our married people have to do, and what the whole Church has to do is ponder in our hearts what sacramental marriage really means. We need to ponder the words of Scripture, spoken so beautifully, so magnificently and so frequently about marriage. Not just on suitable occasions like anniversaries, or weddings, or at a couples' retreat. These words really have to be part of the sacramental life of a couple — so that our couples can deepen their awareness that their way of living with one another is one of the chief forms of catechesis in the Church and is a prime means of evangelisation.

Evangelisation really means we are called to preach and practise love in significant and meaningful ways that touch and affect the lives of all those around us. This is going to be accomplished not just by doing loving things. We ourselves as Church have to be a loving community. To be credible as a Gospel people. Not just as Gospel practitioners. An awful lot of times we separate the book of Scripture from the people of Scripture. We're not called to follow the book, we're called to follow the people of the book. The deeper message we're missing is that the Gospel way of life is to live as a people — his people.

The core of evangelisation, the love experience within our faithful community simply beyond any other love, is that of our sacramental couples. We are tremendously dependent upon our couples not just to do well by one another for their own sake, but to truly love one another so that we can have the hope and conffidence and encouragement to love as a faithful family. What we most have to offer the world is ourselves and a relationship with us. That's the most intimate and most meaningful evangelisation that can be offered. If we just offer the words of the Gospel, we miss the whole point of Jesus' call. Jesus has called us to make him present through our love. In fact, as far as the Church's self-identity is concerned, Matrimony is "the" prime form of catechesis.

This is most evidently true as far as the teaching of children is concerned. How they listen to a homily, how they experience the Eucharist, how they respond to the direction of our Bishops is very much established by the relationship that they had with their parents growing up in the faith.

However, we're raising a point beyond that reality here. We're saying that from adult to adult, the prime way of discovering the inner nature of the Church is through an experience of our sacramental couples loving one another in our name. They reveal that our overriding mission as Catholics is to belong to our fellow

60

Catholics. That it is the life that we establish with one another that creates the Church. For the essential nature of the Sacrament of Matrimony is that a husband and wife have to belong to one another totally and absolutely. Not in deprivation of their individual talents, capabilities and abilities to love, but in celebration of that reality. It's not a giving up or a giving in; it's a giving.

The same thing is true of us as Catholics — that the essential nature of our vocation is to be a community of love, to be totally immersed in one another and to belong to one another. It is that belonging to one another that is the greatest charism that we have to put at the service of this world. It's not a private charism. Just like the Sacrament of Matrimony, the charism of their community life is not just for the two of them, but it is to be spent and missioned to the whole Church. So too, the charism of our belonging to one another as Catholics is to be spent on the whole kingdom.

If we just try to act as individually good people then we deprive the world of our greatest grace which is our relationship with one another. Then we're acting the very way a husband acts who is a pillar of the Church, but ignores his wife. So, we're pillars of the kingdom and we ignore our faith family. We're so busy going about saving the world, we so concentrate on our self-fulfilment, either filling ourselves with Jesus or with knowledge or with personal development, that we're missing the whole point of what our vocation is — which is to be a community of love, which is to be immersed in the life of our fellow believers and to find Jesus in their presence by being present to them.

Now, it is very, very difficult for us to believe that we are a chosen people unless we are witnessing it in the world around us. So the couple's choice of one another is not just important to them, but it is terribly important to us. If our couples aren't continuously re-affirming their choice of one another and really re-choosing one another on a daily basis in love and tenderness, it's going to be very difficult for any of us to really believe that this is what Jesus is doing to us.

That is where the prophetic side of Matrimony keeps coming up. There is no reason why a woman should give her whole being forever to a man, other than that of a free gift. There is no reason why a man should give his whole life and his whole personhood into the care of this woman, and be totally open to her acceptance. There is no reason why Jesus should see me as unique, should have chosen me — other than the fact that he loves me. And that his love is freely given.

So we need to see our couples living out this struggle to choose and to accept the choice in good times and in bad; when it is attractive and when it is not so attracative; when they joyfully accept the choice and when they want to be unchosen, when they want to be independent.

The couple then is the core of any society. In a very real way, a couple in the Sacrament of Matrimony *creates* the Church. Not in the old-fashioned style we used to talk about in terms of building up the body of Christ by having children. That is true, but there is so much more than that. The experience of exclusivity, permanence and unity that sacramental marriage calls us to provides a very secure base upon which the commitment to the Church can be made by all of us. All other human relationships are conditioned to some degree. Matrimony is the only human relationship that is irrevocable, unconditioned, exclusive and above all marked by tenderness and warmth. These are the qualities that are called for in our relationship with the Church.

5

UNITY — OUR SPIRITUALITY

Jesus loves us as he loves his own Body. He gives us his identity. We are no longer our own; we are his. He holds nothing back. He does not keep any part of himself to himself.

It's so hard for us to believe that we are his body. We can take all the theologies about the Body of Christ, about being the people of God, a community of love; we can read them all, we can say all the wonderful words and we can be suitably intellectually impressed, but do we really come away from the Eucharist believing that we in conjunction with our fellow believers are his Body? Do we really act that way? Can we really believe that he makes us one with him?

And yet couples too are called to become bone of each other's bone and flesh of each other's flesh. Couples by being two in one flesh testify to our call to be his body. And to the fact that it is possible. When a loving wife speaks to us, it's like hearing the two of them. A couple should know and understand each other so well that they speak spontaneously on each other's behalf. A beloved takes on the characteristics of a lover.

This is a very, very difficult lesson for us to learn, whether in marriage or in the Church. We have so many things that we consider to be essential to us personally. So many graces that we believe are peculiarly ours. So many talents that we want to exercise, that we just believe that it's unreasonable to put anything above these individual goals of ours or personal calls. We simply have to make an act of faith in the reality that it's the unity that we establish between us whether in Matrimony or in the Church that is our prime charism.

The trouble, though, is that a husband tends to treat his wife just like any other person when it comes to the decisions he makes or the goals that he sets for himself in his life, and so he takes her advice as he would take anyone else's. We do that same thing in the Church. We treat Catholics just like anybody else. Sometimes they're right, sometimes they're wrong. Sometimes they're good, sometimes they're bad. On the other hand, a true husband sees that his wife is in a unique relationship with him and her response to him determines his decisions in life. So too with us and our fellow faithful.

All too often, however, we don't expect very much from marriage. We define our good marriages in terms of what is *not* done. Things like the husband saying, "I don't drink, I don't chase other women, I don't come in late". The wife could be married to a rock for that matter. The rock wouldn't do any of those things either. Or, "I'm a good wife because I take good care of the house, I raise the kids", and so on. A nurse could do that. It says nothing about her relationship with her husband.

Or, at best we think in terms of the individual perfection of the husband or wife. So we can say: "So-and-so is really a good wife", or "He's a good husband". First of all, it's very difficult to understand how somebody can be a great wife if they don't also have a great marriage. For that indicates that we really don't understand what marriage is all about. A person can be a super man, really grace-filled and generous, but unless his wife is enjoying their relationship, then it's hard to see how we can ascribe the title of "great husband" to him. Isn't it really his wife, and what she's experiencing, that determines whether he's a great husband?

Unfortunately, however, we concentrate on the person and not the relationship. We concentrate on the one who is doing the actions rather than the recipient. Maybe a wife took care of a sick husband for twenty years, or he put up with an alcoholic wife for fifteen years and we say: "Gosh, isn't he/she good and wonderful?" That's fair enough; that's okay to say. But when we add the title of the relationship, husband/wife to that statement, then we're not right. We ascribe our judgement in terms of the extraordinary generosity of the *activity*. But marriage is a relationship.

No one is questioning that the woman who took care of her husband for all those years was a very holy woman, but she could have been his cousin. The man who lived with an alcoholic wife

64

for fifteen years could have been doing so in living up to his word and his responsibility with no real relationship with her. In other words, the sanctity was in terms of the deeds that were performed. Someone who wasn't married could have done the same thing.

We simply never talk of holiness in terms of the love relationship that is established between the couple. Yet, that is the root sanctity of any husband and wife. Really, instead of saying "She's such a good wife" the best accolade we could give to her is "Her husband is very happy. He is experiencing the more abundant life that Jesus promised". When we want to ascribe holiness to a man who is a husband, we should say "His wife has the best life of any woman I know. She is loved and loving". But what we tend to do is take their marriage away from them as their focus of holiness. We can ascribe sanctity to a woman who does everything in the parish and is a daily mass and communion goer, or is a pillar of the Church; we can canonise a man who has a passion for justice and a concern for the poor, but they may have no real tenderness in their dealings with one another. In a very real way, we can paraphrase the words of Scripture, "What does it profit a man if he gains the whole world and suffers the loss of his own soul" — What does it profit a man if he loves the whole world and suffers the loss of his wife? The basic spirituality of a husband is to love his wife. The basic holiness of a wife is to tenderise her husband in the Lord. And I don't care what else a man may be; I really can't call him much of a husband, unless he is concentrating on bringing joy and fulfilment to his wife.

In the same way, I don't care what else I am as a Catholic; unless I have a special relationship with my fellow Catholics, I am not much of a Catholic. Just as the prime examination of conscience of a husband has got to be directed to his wife's well-being and happiness, so too, as Catholics we have to face into what the faithful are experiencing of us and how much their life is better because we belong to them. One of the prime calls that I have as a Catholic is to bring joy to my fellow Catholics. That is really ministering to the body of Jesus.

We have the same problem that the Apostles had when Mary Magdalen anointed Jesus' feet with that precious oil. They didn't like the idea at all and they had other suggestions. So too, in the

Church today we have all sorts of other suggestions about how we should spend our resources. But just as Jesus praises Mary Magdalen so he praises us when we anoint his body, our fellow Catholics, with our honest affection, with our devoted attention and our loving concern. This very definitely has to be one of the prime ways in which we serve Jesus in this world today.

Now obviously, a man doesn't just have relationship with his wife; he has relationships with all sorts of other people — children, his own family, neighbours, and so on — but his prime relationship, from which all the others flow, is his relationship with his wife. So we have relationships with non-Christians, with Christians, with people on the street, and so on, but our prime relationship has got to be with our fellow Catholics. Not our exclusive relationship but our prime one. That is that our couples have to witness in their relationship with one another.

Our couples, however, are not just to be nice to each other; they have to become one with one another and identify with one another. It's not just two singles who share responsibilities, privileges, activities and a bedroom. Their whole orientation in life has got to be sharply different from those who are not married. Matrimony is a call to real unity.

One of the difficulties we have is that we tend to see the ideal marriage as one in which this man and this woman mutually satisfy one another and each of them get out of the relationship what they want. That's not a unifying love at all. That's not the kind of marriage that we're talking about in the Sacrament of Matrimony. What that is basically is two people who are living together in mutual peace and harmony. That's fine and it's good. But we're looking for much more than that in this Sacrament. We should see that this is a whole new way of life they're called to. There has to be a couple awareness of life rather than a heightened, improved individual awareness.

That beautiful, beautiful wedding homily which calls to our couples to become one in mind, one in heart, one in affection — you know, we think that sounds nice: "Isn't that a lovely thing to say at a wedding! Whoever thought of that, he was really a sort of poet". But that isn't just a kind of hallmark card in ecclesiastical terms. That's a real mission that our couples have to live out on a day-to-day basis. We don't take that seriously enough. All too often we encourage our couples: "Look, as long as you put the meals on the table, babe, as long as you don't knock him too often with your tongue, as long as you come home every night and listen to her at least sometimes, then, you are all right". No, they are not all right. I mean *they* may be satisfied but they're *our* Sacrament, not their own alone. The Sacrament of Matrimony is a Sacrament of the whole Church. Therefore in a very special way the couple who is sacramental is ordained to us and belongs to us.

So we need much more from couples than just a mutual compatibility. We really need them to be working on a daily basis, to become one in mind, to think alike. Not simply because it helps make things go smoother around the house, but because it's their vocation. We are calling them to give a lot, but we're not asking them to be reduced, we're not asking them to become less themselves. We are asking them to consciously and deliberately work on becoming unified.

He says: "Oh, I have my ideas and she has her ideas". Well, that was fine until you got married. Now you have got to work on having *our* ideas and the point is not "Will you succeed totally?" but "Are you working at it?"

The problem is that she is attracted to unity as long as it's her unity. He reckons it's wonderful when they think alike as long as she thinks his way. Or they excuse themselves on the basis that it is not going to happen every day. Fine, but the more they excuse themselves, then it comes about that it doesn't happen any day.

That doesn't mean that either of them fakes it or just becomes a wishy-washy piece of putty. But it does mean that they have to be aiming at seeking to become unified in their thoughts. He has to be reaching out to her, she has to be striving with him so that they're not just two separate people in their mental approach to things, but that they really are a couple interiorly as well as exteriorly.

Unity is something that they eagerly desire until they see what it really is. They simply want a unity of feelings; he wants to feel close to her, she wants to feel warm toward him and to feel his tenderness toward her. They limit unity to that. But unity is much more powerful and much more meaningful than simply that of feelings. The feelings are an outgrowth of the other unity and they're beautiful and good and nobody is cutting them down. But, they can't define the unity that they're called to in the Sacrament of Matrimony in terms only of how they feel about one another on any given occasion. Because they can't control their feelings. Feelings come and go. A Sacrament has to be much more firmly planted. We are called to be unified in our thoughts.

If you think that it's difficult for a couple to overcome their selfishness and their egoism and their stubborn sticking to their own opinions, how much more difficult is it for us as a Church community? We simply have to be led into this by our matrimonied couples in the Church, because, by ourselves, judging by the evidence of recent years, we're not going to get there. Each of us digs our heels in and wants it our way and we keep thinking our way is best and we miss the fact that unity is a higher priority than our own convictions.

That's a hard pill to swallow because it goes against the whole sense of individualism that is so dominant in the Church today. It seems to be attacking personal integrity. Actually it's not. If I gave up my own way of looking at something because I was forced to, or out of fear because somebody made themselves superior to me, or out of my own weakness, then yes, it would be definitely attacking my personal integrity. But this is a gift of love. So I reach out to what the other person believes, not because I find the belief so attractive but because I find the other person so attractive. That's what marriage can teach us. That's one of the prime witnesses that our sacramental couples can offer us in the Church today. Boy, is it badly needed!

The point here is not simply respecting each other's values. It's not a question of: "Does she have her things that she considers important?" and "I'll let her do her thing, as long as she let's me do my thing". Rather, it's a question of working hard to establish the same priorities in our value system and to develop the same goals.

For in the Church today, we're going in 75 different directions at once. And we don't care what our fellow Catholics are doing as long as their values don't interfere with our values. If I establish myself as myself alone, and I'm only concerned about you and the

Church if you're interfering with me — or as a control on myself if I'm interfering with you — then what kind of family is that? What kind of pilgrim people do we have? We're not a pilgrim people at all; we're a mass of pilgrims. We can take something beautiful like that statement of Vatican II about being a pilgrim people, and miss the real beauty of it. It's a pilgrim *people;* it's not just pilgrim. Being a people is the essential note of that. So we simply have to experience the lived out recognition of our married couples that principles don't outweigh relationship. The overriding concern that we have to have is for one another.

The grace of unity, moreover, is not for his sake or her sake; it's for them as a couple. The grace to speak as a couple to the whole Church — not as a single person. There are plenty of beautiful single persons around doing that. Married people shouldn't poach on their territory. They are supposed to be speaking as a couple. No, it doesn't always mean that both have to be physically present, but each has to be speaking the other at all times. So that the graces of the Sacrament of Matrimony come to each party in, with and through the other party.

An important part of their unity, too, is to really be in love and to become one in affection. Too often, couples say: "Oh, we had that when we were dating, now we have a more mature life". The answer is "I'm sorry for your trouble. Why don't you get immature again? You might be closer to God." You see, the thing is — as soon as they don't feel affectionate, then they stop being affectionate. "Well, affection isn't something you can fake," they say. No, but it is something they can do anytime they choose. It doesn't have to be something automatic, like they did when they were dating and he couldn't keep his hands off her.

Even in human terms, the quality of a couple's whole relationship is going to be sharply improved, the more affectionate they are toward one another — not only doing the right thing for one another, but doing it gently and tenderly. But more importantly, how can we expect to have affection for our fellow Catholics, if our Sacraments of Matrimony are not affectionate? The vast majority of the adult Church is married. There is a tenderness, a gentleness in relationship when they are physically affectionate with one another, which carries over to the whole community.

They as married couples can establish an environment and an atmosphere in which this happens to us without our even recognising it.

Have you ever seen an old married couple that have been married for forty or fifty years? Did you ever notice how they look physically alike — and part of it is the shrinkage of old age. They take on each other's smile lines and frown lines and their faces become a map of their life together. Now, if that can happen physically, it can also happen interiorly in mind and heart and will. And that is what we are called to be as Church, not physical look-alikes, but interior look-alikes. We are called to be one with one another. Not just to enjoy closeness when it happens or to pray desperately that our disagreements will pass. We're called to concretely do all in our power under the light of grace to become one in mind, one in heart, one in affection with our fellow Catholics. This is a faith family, and we have to become familied with our people.

Such extraordinary unity is the vocation of a sacramental couple. Not as a fleeting experience. You know, a lot of people say: "We had great moments". "Oh, yeah, I can recall, there were times when I felt I was inside him," or "I discovered that our hearts were beating together." And that's wonderful and that's not to be discouraged. What we are saying is that that should be a way of life — not an incidental oasis along the way.

We are the body of Jesus and the body must be in harmony with itself. Each individual part cannot be about accomplishing it's own purposes, trying to get along with Jesus instead of becoming one with him. There is a unity that we have to have with our fellow Catholics that we're simply not facing today. And husbands and wives have the most experience in our midst of getting beyond that type of egoism. We're not trying to canonise them or say they always do this or that some couples ever do this. We are saying that as a faith family, that's what we have to call our sacramental couples to accomplish with one another, and then we have to listen to the prophecy that their accomplishment of unity with one another gives to us. We cannot allow Sacraments to just accept the whole thrust of the world's plan for marrieds today — to establish two individual sovereignties which try to get along like friendly neighbours.

For the Sacrament of Matrimony is not living just like everybody else lives, except that you are happier at it; it is a totally different way of life with a completely different set of values. Jesus said, "That they may be one as you and I are one". That is his vision for the whole Church. And the sign of his vision for the whole Church is how our matrimonied couples are living with one another. Is their unity something that people just don't understand? It puzzles them. It might even turn them off. For the real condemnation is not that people say: "You're acting different!" The real condemnation is that people don't see any difference and they think you're just as nice as everybody else. You may go to the the wrong Church on Sunday, but other than that . . . .

We fear Jesus, of course. We don't really believe that if we put ourselves in his hands to become one with him, we will be fully happy. So we need our couples to convince us, to call us forth from our selfish fears. We need our husbands to show us, by the way we live, that they believe that their wives care for them even more than they care for themselves, that in her hands he is better off than he is in his own. We need to see the husband treat his wife as he treats his own body, with the same tenderness and the same overriding concern. We need to see a wife who really wants to understand her husband even more than she wants to be understood by him. We are called to put on Christ and if that seems impossible (and maybe, if we are honest with ourselves, undesirable because we see self-suppression as a problem), it's because we haven't experienced couples who find their fullness in putting one another first.

Another way we need our couples to call us to unity is in their matrimonial prayer. Not just the prayer of the married, but specifically marital prayer. Certainly one of the things we find most endearing in Scripture is that statement of Jesus "Where two or three are gathered in my name there I am in the midst of them". What better example of two being gathered together in his name than a Sacrament of Matrimony?

Couples gathering together in his name, of course, can't be just the couple going to Mass together, although that is certainly very

71

good. But why do they simply have to pray privately, alone? We are not asking here that they shouldn't pray ever individually. What we are saying is, though, that there is also a definitive need on their part and on the part of the Church for couples to start praying to the Lord together as a couple.

An awful lot of times a husband or wife may know that their spouse is a very faithful person, a true believer, a very prayerful person, but they haven't experienced that prayerfulness, or it has only touched them intermittently. All they know about their spouse is that he or she does pray, and does pray very meaningfully, and it is of great importance, but they have never been exposed to that prayer. Isn't that a shame? Why can't a husband and wife go to the Lord together?

He hasn't called them to come to him alone in prayer. They need to come to him with their love, this man, this woman. This applies whether they are praying alone as individuals or whether they are praying together as a couple. They can't go as unmarried just because they happen to be talking to the Lord individually; they are going with their husband or with their wife, even when he or she is not physically present.

This is one of the richnesses of the Church that we haven't experienced — and that we need. This is something that would bring the husband and wife together and help them to appreciate each other and be more responsive to one another. Certainly they can't have a sacramental life without a prayer life. But if their Sacrament is their coupleness, then they should also have a prayerfulness that is centred around their relationship with one another.

Moreover the direction their prayer takes and the areas of concentration in their prayer life should be about their marriage. All too often couples go to the Lord in terms of themselves as individual persons, in terms of their personal relationship with him, or the needs of their children or the needs of this world. But the overriding concern of a husband and wife has got to be their relationship with one another. That is what he has called them to do.

So a couple needs to pray to Jesus to give them some of the desire he has for them in their marriage. And some of the real passion for one another. They need to pray to be sexy. Not just to be more long suffering, more patient. No woman wants to be married to a long suffering man. That long suffering man makes her suffer more than he ever does. No man wants to be married to a patient sexless woman — I mean, he could be married to a doll. A doll never gets upset and is certainly sexless. But we don't go and pray for things like that. We see sex as a human thing. It's not something that should be a subject of prayer; it's simply not spiritual enough. An awful lot of husbands and wives make the intimacy of their flesh experience with one another something that is apart from the spirituality of their relationship. Or they think that sex has to be earned by the rest of the relationship instead of seeing that it has to be an integrated whole and that the flesh is as holy as the spirit and that conversation is no better a means of building up a relationship than sex is.

And yet the fact of the matter is that husband and wife are called in their marriage primarily to make their spouse happy. To fill them with the light and life that Jesus wants for them. Certainly one of the best ways for a husband or wife to accomplish this in their spouse is through their sexual experience with one another. This is a God-given gift. It is part of the whole sacramental experience. It simply must not be reduced to just a human experience. Jesus is as much interested in our couples' sexual experience of one another as any other aspect — in fact, more so, because he recognises that so many of the other difficulties that they discover in their marriage will be overcome if they can only be passionate toward one another. Sex should be a frequent subject of their prayers. They must pray constantly to be more effective and more meaningful in their sexual love for their spouses.

But even if we accept that a couple should be praying together, we haven't really accepted the fact that the love relationship in human terms between husband and wife is truly spiritual. That their unity is their spirituality. We recognise that it is good, but I don't think we really see it as a prayer. If somebody comes up to us and asks us good ways to pray, we seldom even think to ask them if they're married. We tend to give them good ways to pray and say it applies across the board. But it really doesn't. We simply haven't developed ways of matrimonial spirituality. We've given our couples spirituality that is fundamentally baptismal and then

73

have them fit that into the circumstances of their marriage. We miss the whole point that their marriage is the sanctifying event and it is their marriage that is to be enhanced.

So, for example, instead of telling a husband to meditate over Scriptures, what we might do is to tell him to spend an hour really listening to his wife. That would be a tremendous prayer. We might tell a wife to pray for passion, not just that she not refuse her husband but that she positively and joyfully engage herself in their sexual relationship. Sex very definitely is a prayer. We might tell a woman to really spend some time and care over the meals she serves.

We look on these as good activities, of course, and we have no objection to suggesting them, but we don't think of them in the context of prayer as such. That's because of our narrow vision of what prayer is. Because we have a sense of prayer being a private thing between Jesus and myself and we haven't recognised that the call to relationship is our basic call and that Matrimony is above all the Sacrament of relationship and therefore the model of who we are to be with one another with Jesus. And until we recognise that this call to unity is the basic spirituality of the couple, we will continue to denude our couples, to impoverish the entire Church and to miss the point of our own spirituality.

The call to unity, of course, is not something abstract — it is a call to intimacy. There is a very personal kind of love which Jesus has for us. Scripture says: "He pitched his tent among us". He took on our life. He made himself one of us. He no longer lived on his terms. He took on our way of living. He wants to be totally *intimate* with us. He wants to become a complete part of our life and to flesh himself in us. His selection of us is not strictly in terms of the things that he does for us or what he asks us to do for him, but he wants to get inside us and us inside him. He wants us no longer to be separate but to live his life. That is what intimacy is.

This quality of intimacy can be very much applied to married couples. But it isn't just in their saying that they love one another. That's nice. Nor is it in all the sweet little things that they do for one another. There has to be much more than that. A total intimacy. A real understanding and sense of closeness that he or she really cares. He has to find his life in her. She has to be open and to be totally involved in his way of being. There can be no part of them that they keep to themselves. Marriage is a complete personal involvement. It's not selective openness. It's not partial responsiveness. I keep nothing of me to me. I'm interested and I'm alert to every part of my spouse. I let that other person into my most secret thoughts and desires and awareness.

This is very hard to do. We're always trying to keep parts of ourselves to ourselves, just in case something happens, or we're fearful that the other person will use it against us, or it will turn off the other person, or we won't keep our own identity, or whatever the excuse is that we use. But the fact is that the Sacrament of Matrimony is a call to be total with one another, not just total in the sense of doing the right things or not violating our vows or not displeasing one another, but to really give our whole selves into the hands of the other person, to take on a common life together.

That's a process, of course; that's not something that's ever accomplished. Yes, there will be failures and out of those failures will come hurts, but our goal as a husband and wife is to be totally intimate with one another, to fully belong to one another. Unfortunately, most husbands and wives rate their marriage in terms of the activities that they perform for one another and how well they live up to their duties rather than in terms of the level of intimacy that they have achieved. In a lot of marriages, there just isn't enough intimacy. They restrict their intimacy to sex. But the truth of the matter is a couple can have sex every night and never really be intimate. Sex in itself is not necessarily intimate. It can be an expression of an intimacy but unfortunately it can often be merely private actions. Sex can be engaged in even by good husbands and wives as strictly for the activity in itself and not for the purpose of getting to know each other better or communicating on a deeper level with one another.

Of course, it isn't even a question of the sexual experience in marriage. Couples can live with one another for years and never really know one another. How many husbands have said: "My wife doesn't understand me"? How many wives have complained about loneliness? This is a heartfelt expression of the lack of intimacy that they are experiencing.

Too often husbands and wives have categories of their lives, and sometimes whole areas of their lives where they are more intimate with their mother than with their husband, or more open with their buddies than with their wives. In other areas of their lives they are more intimate with their children than with their spouse. They believe they get more understanding sometimes or that they can talk about certain subjects more easily with these other people than they can with their spouse. Naturally in the beginning of a marriage that is probably true because they have more practice with a mother than with a husband. They have more experience with a buddy than with a wife. That's what has to go. It's not easy; it's not something that we wave a magic wand and it happens. We have to gradually eradicate those habits and train ourselves to believe that our calling is to find more understanding, more responsiveness in our spouse than in anybody else. That can only happen if we're completely ourselves with our beloved wife or husband. The point, of course, is not to reduce our intimacy with other people. An intimate relationship is always very precious and very beautiful and so there's nothing wrong with maintaining and increasing that kind of relationship with a member of the family or a friend. The point we're trying to raise here is that the greatest intimacy of all should be accomplished with a spouse.

It is the same type of intimacy that Jesus has with his body. He has an intimacy with the Church, just like the intimacy between a husband and wife which is totally unique — and it is a flesh intimacy. He became man. He took on flesh. He was conceived by the Holy Spirit, born of the Virgin Mary, so as to become one with us. Specifically in the flesh. The favourite title he gave himself was Son of Man. He revelled in being fleshed. In Matrimony the total relationship obviously transcends the flesh but is very much rooted in it. The same thing is true in our relationship with Jesus which calls us to fleshed intimacy in his body, the Church. Our very call to relate to him is a call to relate to these people.

We have such a great deal of difficulty with a fleshed God. We want to throw away the body, the Church, and go directly to Jesus. That is why we want to be vague "Christians" instead of Catholics. Essentially we want to be non-denominational. We are afraid of intimacy.

76

That's why we need couples. To call us away from non-denominationalism and from a spiritualised Jesus to a fleshed intimacy with his Church. The whole notion of sacramental marriage is to witness to the beauty and holiness of the Incarnation. The flesh of his intimacy. Our husbands and wives have to be models to us. They have to witness to us that the kind of life that Jesus wants us to have in him is not something that lessens us or reduces us but actually enhances our whole way of being. They have to call us to fidelity.

Unfortunately, we tend to think of fidelity as staying out of somebody else's bed. But true fidelity is much more than that. It is enjoying the one that they're in. That is much harder. There are a lot of good men and women who would never think of sleeping around, but there is no joy in their sexual experience with one another. That is infidelity. For full fidelity calls us to be continuously increasing our delight in one another sexually and making that joy and happiness so evident to our spouse that it is part of their fullness in life.

Of course, something like this doesn't just happen. All we have to do is to look around us to see that in so many marriages the fire goes out after a certain number of years. Oh they definitely continue to love one another and they're very thoughtful and helpful toward one another and they provide a certain amount of companionship, but the passion has dribbled away over the years. They have lost or at least sharply diminished the quality of being irresistible to one another. They fall into the trap of getting used to one another and start to live a brother and sister relationship with suitable sexual intimacy. They sometimes even think the loss of that passion is a good thing and shows that their love is much more real and much more spiritual. Quite the contrary is true.

For Jesus' love is a passionate one. He didn't just not betray his disciples. He positively affirmed them and chose them and delighted in being with them. That is the way Jesus is for us too. "With desire have I desired to eat this meal with you," he said. The yearning that is within him. It is just not in terms of "We'll have a good meal together," or "Well, we've been together for three years, so who else would I be with?" No: "With desire have I desired to be with you." There's no sense of the old shoe there.

77

Jesus is telling us that he's passionately involved, that his feelings and emotions are very much a part of his choice of us, telling us how irresistible he finds us. And that is the call that our husbands and wives have towards one another — to delight in each other. To reveal that yearning that Jesus has for the Church. The Church needs our married couples to be obviously *in love* with one another as well as loving toward one another. Jesus told us, "I tell you these things that my joy may be in you and your joy may be complete. I have come that you may have life and have it more abundantly". If sacramental marriage just comes across to people as dull and unenthusiastic, where is the sign? The love-relationship between a sacramental couple can't just be good; it has to be shown as attractive.

People in general expect young love. What they do not really expect is passionate devoted enthusiastic married love. That's what we have to establish as a true witness sign in the Church. For example, we have to make married sex so much better than any other kind of sex. We can use all the philosophical arguments and theological arguments in the world that sex should be reserved for marriage, we can talk reason until we're blue in the face, but the really believable call to marital love is when married sex is obviously different and better than any other kind of sex. That's what our couples have to offer.

We tend to resist this. We tend to say, "Oh my God, there's so much more to marriage than that!" We're not denying that at all. That's definitely true. But because there are other dimensions to marriage doesn't deny that sex is an essential aspect of marriage. And all the other beautiful things about marriage do not excuse a lack of ambition for their sexual relationship with one another. The point is not either/or: it's both/and. Just as sex by itself can never be a replacement for all the other beautiful marital experiences, so too, no matter how well a couple may be doing with one another in all other areas of married life, that is no substitute for a vibrant sexual experience of each other. That is true on a personal level between husband and wife, but it is even more true on the sacramental level as far as the Church's stake in a husband-wife relationship is concerned. There is nothing that will attract more attention and more positive response on the part of those both inside and outside the Church than to see that our matrimonied couples continue to grow over the years and increase their passionate love towards one another.

A lover is not one who does good things because he is so good; he does them because he is so much in love, because he sees his beloved as so good. That is a sign that not only is Jesus so overwhelmingly good, but that he is in love with us because he finds us, the Church, so tremendously attractive. The sign the couple should be is not just to do good things for one another but having those good things drawn out of the man or the woman by the attractiveness of his or her spouse.

The same thing is true in our relationship with the fellow members of our Church. All too often we are very dutiful toward that Church. We would never think of missing Mass on Sunday. We do what the Bishop asks us to do. We send our kids to Catholic School. All those dutiful things. And I am not saying that we should not do them. But, is there any joy in our being Catholic? Or is it just a responsibility I live up to? More important, do I have any joy in Catholics? Do I find myself particularly attracted to them? If I do not find the body of Jesus attractive, then how am I finding him attractive? How am I really relating to him as he wants? In a way, it's the reverse of the traditional feminine cry — "you only love me for my body" — Jesus can say equally to us, "You only love me without my body". He's pleading with us: "I don't want you just to love me for what I did 2,000 years ago; I don't want you just to love me for my mind; I don't want you just to love me for my spirit. I want you to love the whole of me. I want you to love my body, your fellow Catholics, and it is your joy in them and your enthusiasm in being bodied with me through them that most rejoices me."

So being part of the Church is really a call to being in love with the other members of the Church. Not just to get along with them; not just to do things with them. Enjoying one another in the Church is more important than "keeping the faith". For to be a faithful Catholic is not merely to do Catholic things loyally and frequently. It is not just to hold to a set of principles. It is really to be *in love* with our fellow Catholics, to rejoice in one another.

That's a tough one, of course. How can I be in love with someone I don't find attractive? Well, we have to change — not our fellow Catholics but ourselves. It's just like the man to whom his wife is not beautiful. What has to change is how he sees her. The problem is not her objective beauty or lack of beauty; the problem is in his eyesight. Even believing she is beautiful will make her beautiful. After all, nobody wants to be loved with a cold decision — we have to learn from our couples that we need to decide to look for the goodness in each other. So too, in the way we respond to our fellow Catholics — we have to allow the Lord to work on us to get us to see them with his eyes.

But then there is so much we have to learn from our prophetic couples. Their love for one another is the most magnificent power they have and the greatest parable in the world. And above all, it is this relationship with one another, their own unity, their being in love, that is their basic spiritual life, their fundamental prayer. And ours too.

Unity, after all, is our most basic call. And it is the grace of unity that the couple is above all graced with. So the matrimonial graces are not just for the husband and wife alone, but for the whole Church. That unity would be nice for the couple who are merely married. For the sacramental couple it's essential. Not for their sake, but for ours.

6

SIGNS COVERED, SIGNS DENIED

The Sacraments, the sacramental couples, are a sign. Now the most outstanding facet about a sign is that it communicates. The material of a sign may have no importance in itself, such as a highway road sign. It is just a rectangular piece of wood or metal. It is the message on it that is important. On the other hand, the sign in itself *can* be important. For example, an invitation which is very carefully done indicates the importance of the event to which I am invited and the value the sender places on it. Or a sign may also indicate the importance of the person who receives the sign. For example, a letter may be handwritten, rather than typed, or a present may be particularly expensive or very carefully thought out to match the person to whom it is given.

All these aspects of signs are most explicitly fulfilled in Jesus. His personhood indicates the importance our Father places on our adoption. Jesus also indicates by his very being how valued we are by our Father. In his very being he calls prime attention to the message he contains — that we are saved because we are loved and lovable.

A Sacrament, though, is one step beyond a sign, because it not only brings the message, but it also effects the message. For example, Baptism not only signifies death and resurrection and cleansing, but it brings it about. So Jesus is the ultimate Sacrament truly. He not only brought the message of salvation from our Father and the statement about our adoption, but he accomplished that salvation through his death and resurrection.

All Sacraments are acts of Jesus. Each Sacrament in its own way creates the reality of Jesus' presence in our midst. So Baptism is the sign of salvation by incorporation into the body of Jesus. The Sacrament of penance is the sign of our reconciliation with our

Father, that our sins have been forgiven. The Sacrament of Matrimony signifies the reality of Jesus' relationship with his special people, the Church, and creates that reality of the love of a man and a woman, which speaks out how Jesus and the Church relate to one another.

I think we can say that there is no love on the face of this earth like the love of a man and woman in marriage. It is absolutely unique. Therefore, the choice of that sign was a particularly appropriate one. It makes it very clear that the dominant note Jesus wishes to reveal to us about our treatment of the Church, our fellow believers is one of tenderness.

All the externals of the Sacraments are normal things, like water and oil. Marriage is certainly normal and human too. Now, obviously, dirty water could be used for Baptism, but it would really take something away from the sign value, wouldn't it? The same thing is true for oil that is rancid. Consequently, we must see how terribly vital it is that the sign of Matrimony, the love of a husband and wife for one another speak the warmth and affection that Jesus has for the Church. All of us have to have the same reverence for the sacramental sign of the couple that we have for these other signs. In fact, much more, because actually the sign of the baptismal water is only there when the actual Baptism is taking place. When it is being stored, it is not the baptismal sign.

In a very real way the Sacrament of Matrimony is like the Sacrament of the Eucharist. The Eucharist is not just the Sacrament at the moment of consecration. Neither is Matrimony just a Sacrament at the moment of the exchange of vows. The Sacrament of Matrimony is always present in the continuing renewal of commitment to one another in the lived out life and love of the couple. Therefore, couples in the Church should be particularly revered, not in terms of superiority to any other person in the Church, but in terms of the sign that their relationship is to the Church and to the world.

One of the things we have to remember, of course, as far as the Sacraments are concerned is that it isn't just the externals that create the Sacrament. It is also very much the internals. The recipient of the Sacrament has to intend to be receiving it. The minister of the Sacrament has to be intending at least to do what the Church desires to be done. The fact that a couple are married and living together in peace and harmony and enjoy one another doesn't really make them sacramental. They have to *intend* to be. Just as water is not in itself a sign of Baptism, so marriage in itself is not a sign of Christ's relationship with his Church. It has to be deliberately chosen that way — we are not a sacramental sign just because we are married in a Church building. And since the Sacrament is a continuing one, that intention has to be continuous too.

Naturally, of course, this sign has to be based on the tender love, affection and desire for unity by husband and wife with one another, but it must go beyond that. Otherwise it is a non-committal sign. So the couple has to speak this sign to one another, but they also have to speak this sign to the whole Church. Therefore, it has to be very much their concern how their relationship is appearing to others. Is it truly signifying Jesus' relationship with the Church?

The difficulty with the people of the Church who are experiencing this Sacrament is that they have been concentrating on doing it right, that is, doing the husband and wife thing right, and letting the sign take care of itself. Their concentration has been on being a better person in marriage, rather than on the coupleness which is the marriage. Even sincerely religious couples often haven't had that much concern as to how visible the sign of their love for one another was to the Church. They leave it up to others to notice, or hope that people experience it for themselves. Too often marriage among Catholics can lead to a good human relationship. It certainly isn't to be scorned that they do better with one another and are more aware of Church things. But we are not sacramentally effective, if our sign value is not really coming across to those whose lives we touch.

Our good people just don't see their marriage as that valuable. They think that because they are married that they just don't have that much relevance to the Church, or that they have a relevance to the Church as individuals, not specifically as married. Thanks be to God we have increasing emphasis today on the importance of the laity to the well-being of the whole Church but we haven't distinguished the laity who committed themselves to the sacramental way of Matrimony and those who are living in our baptismal and confirmation way of life. It isn't that one is better than the other, but they are very definitely different and we simply have to begin to establish a real awareness that Matrimony is a whole different way of life. We can't just clump all the laity together as a group.

Our couples, however, are simply not being called to this. The homilies don't concentrate on things like this. The groups we've formed, prayer groups and things like that just ignore the Sacrament of Matrimony. We tend not to look on Matrimony as a particular charism that should be spent. In a very real way, we're crippled in the Church. We're living a Church life in which only three Sacraments are lived — Baptism, Confirmation and the Eucharist.

A perfect example of the tragic way that we approach people is when young couples who are seriously dating or are engaged ask the question, "Why do we have to wait for our sexual experience of one another until after we're married?" And, we go through all sorts of convoluted argumentation how such conduct will have an impact on them personally — which very frequently is unconvincing to say the least. But we never bring the relationship with the Church in. We're not talking Church rules on sin here but fidelity to us and our values; we simply don't recognise the deep personal involvement that we as Church have in the Sacrament of Matrimony.

Furthermore, our good couples just haven't had the question posed to them: "What is the difference between their marriage as members of the Church, and the marriage of two good people who love one another and do well with one another, and have no relationship at all with the Church?" In other words, "What is the difference between marriage and Matrimony?" Unless our own people see that there has to be a difference, then how could we possibly expect those outside the Church to experience any difference? It would, in all probablility, be very difficult even for our best and most sincere, knowledgeable and spiritual couples to be able to define in terms of their marriage, not in terms of their personhood, what the difference is between them married in the Church and another good couple with or without faith who has no Church involvement and experience. Those differences can't be solely in terms of baptismal and confirmation experiences and responsibilities. Otherwise, how is Matrimony a Sacrament any more than parenthood is, or friendship, or religious life, all of which are close interpersonal relationships between baptised people?

Jesus, after all, called us to belong to him and to be his body. That calls us to be set apart. Now, I don't think that most married people take themselves apart from general society. They have the same value system as everybody else in society, whether they are married or unmarried. In our society, leisure time is a way of life now. And if couples are going to live leisure time focused on adult activities, they can't be family-oriented no matter how many children they have. They may have 13 children, but the children have to fit into their orientation in life.

And I don't think that the matrimonied couple consider themselves apart from non-sacramental marriage. I don't mean segregated, or looking down on. But do they have a different value system? The value system that we are called to in the Sacrament of Matrimony is to be one in mind, one in heart, one in affection. It's not just to have a good marriage, maybe not to fight too much, to raise good kids, and have adequate money to retire on.

We're facing a crisis of faith specifically on that question, for within the community of the faithful there is also a great deal of indifference towards one another. Just as there is little sense of the difference between Matrimony and marriage, neither in our consciousness does there seem to be any sense that we have a special call to one another or that we have a unique relationship that we are to establish with one another. As long as we don't see anything unique and special about it then we're not going to act in any special way towards one another and, therefore, we make Jesus less visible, we make the building of the kingdom less possible.

Matrimony is supposed to exhibit the special relationship Jesus has with his Church. If that relationship is just that we do more married things — the same things that everybody else does — or if we just do them in an improved manner, then the whole picture doesn't hold water. Or we have to say that St. Paul really didn't mean it when he held out sacramental marriage as a revealer of the relationship that Jesus has with his Church. Certainly, we don't want to hold either of these things.

No, Matrimony is a sign, and a sign offers information that people can find useful or helpful or necessary. But it has to be visible. If it is covered over or inaccessible or overshadowed, it simply does not communicate. In which case, it exists, but it's not meaningful. It's like driving along the highway and you are looking for an exit sign and a branch has grown over it, and the highway department when you call in your complaint say: "But the sign is there". A lot of good that does you!

And the fact is that we have covered over our Sacraments of Matrimony. First of all with rituals. We have reduced Matrimony to a priest and two witnesses and of course a couple. And as long as that is taken care of, you've got a Sacrament — when actually we only have the beginnings of a Sacrament; we are only starting out on our way.

For one of the beautiful images that came out of Vatican II was that we are a pilgrim people. It attacked the whole notion of triumphalism and the idea that we had it made or that we really knew what it was to be God's chosen people. It very clearly proclaimed to us that we were working things out; that we didn't really know our way — that we were *on* our way. This is another beautiful reason why Matrimony is such an excellent sign of the Church. We all recognise that marriage isn't accomplished just because a couple fall in love and decide to get married and actually go through with it. It's a whole process that is life long and there are many false starts and there are many dead ends that we have to get ourselves out of. Marriage is truly a pilgrimage. But a pilgrimage of love. And the important point is not where we get to; it's that we go together lovingly. That's exactly what we should be aiming at in the Church.

There has been altogether too much concentration on the wedding ceremony up to now. Whereas, Matrimony is not a past event that the couple is living out. It is a present reality. And the marrying has to be constant. It has to be a daily amen to each other.

One of the reasons why marriage becomes dull and stale and a certain routine sets in is that they're living out a past commitment instead of making a present one. They have stopped growing together.

Similarly, we have a tendency to believe that being Catholic is a static state too. That I'm as Catholic today as I'm ever going to be. And if I just maintain that level, I'll be all right. Just like in marriage, that's not adequate. As a 20-year-old, yes, a husband's love is complete if he gives it completely to his wife. But as a 40-year-old, he can't give her a 20-year-old love — that's just not adequate any more. She's more and he's more. The same thing is true as far as our relationship with the Church is concerned. After 40 years of being a Catholic, I should be better at it. In other words, I should be more in relationship with that Catholic faith community than I was 15 years ago. I should know my fellow Catholics better and be more aware of them.

The second thing we have covered over Matrimony with is "motherhood". The real basic reason is that we just don't like flesh and we are very, very tacky about accepting a real man and woman relationship. Sex is evidently an essential note of the marital relationship. Marriage is so obviously an experience of the body. Obviously, it's much more than that, but it definitely is a body experience. This is one of the reasons why we have had so much difficulty in proclaiming the sacramentality of this experience. We really have a problem with the Incarnation. We don't like a flesh God and we don't like anything that speaks so obviously of flesh. Maybe that's why Jesus chose Matrimony. He said: "Listen, I'm going to do my thing, not your thing, and you will take my terms, not yours. After all, you are my Church".

It is very interesting that in the Church we tend to disapprove if a mother and father leave their child with a babysitter overnight, but we have no problem with a husband being away four nights in a row. Which shows that parenthood, and particularly motherhood — but not marriage — is where our interests lie. We feel very ill-at-ease with the idea of the mother being away a lot. The real concentration is on the mother. We're really not as much concerned about the father being away. Yeah, we'd like him home, but the mother-child relationship is the dominant relationship in our minds.

Actually, the dominant relationship has got to be the husband-wife relationship. Not that there is any rejection of the maternity involved here, but there is no mother without a father (even for the single parent). Too often we reduce family to a Madonna type of thing and we take away the marital relationship. We focus strictly on the parental one and most especially on the maternal parent. We are much more comfortable with a parental love than we are with a marital one. So, very soon after their marriage, as soon as a child comes along, we concentrate on their parenthood rather than on their relationship with one another. The dominant theme, not only in the way we talk to them, but in the way we think about them is in terms of the relationship with the child and very definitely we think of it in terms of two individuals, mother-father, relating individually to the child. We do not see that the way the child should be treated is in terms of their coupleness rather than in terms of their parenthood.

The one absolutely unique quality that the man/woman relationship has above all others, of course, is the capability to introduce new life into this world and into the Church. And this is a very real part of the imaging of God. One of the distinguishing characteristics of God as God in his creative power. And when that power with which our couples are graced is rejected and suppressed, looked upon as irrelevant or a burden, the revelation of who God is is diminished in this world and specifically in our midst in the Church.

It's important, however, to stress again that it's the couple that is the image of this creative God. Not the mother. The whole question of the grace of *parenthood* being an aspect of the Sacrament of Matrimony is something that's being very sadly bypassed in the Church today. It's a singles mentality that couples have. The graces of the Sacrament of Matrimony are never given to an individual person as such for his or her personal well-being, but always to couples and for the sake of their coupleness. The capability of being a parent is one of the really deep graces of the Sacrament of Matrimony, but that goes through one person to the other.

The only way, for example, that a man ever even knows he's a father is if his wife tells him. Unfortunately, she doesn't always. She says: *"I'm* pregnant". But paternity is just as real as maternity and we don't recognise it. It is really an act of faith on the part of a man to believe that he is pregnant. And he is — just as much as the woman is. He goes through the same agony, the same worries, the same concerns, the same fears. Is there something in my seed that is going to hurt that child? Is the child going to be healthy? Will I live long enough to raise that child? Am I going to be a good father or am I going to be like all the other guys on the block? The whole thing. You see, a man can only accept his fatherhood by his wife's prophecy.

Furthermore, it's a tough thing to believe that a man has anything to do with it all. It's so obviously a feminine thing. Whereas maternity, in fact, is a gift from the husband. The wife takes it as *her* gift and that's why we have trouble. The whole point of being a mother is to prophesy that he is a father. Not just during the course of pregnancy, but through her whole life. What happens is that even with the LeMans method, which is a very good thing, we get the guy involved but in terms of supporting *her* pregnancy. When are we going to recognise *his?*

So too, with being a Catholic. Just as a woman has to say: "How am I doing in my pregnancy for his fatherhood?" We have to ask ourselves: "How am I doing with our love-relationship to advance the Church?" Not, "How am I growing in my spiritual life?" not, "How am I growing in my concern for the poor in my Apostolate?" But "Is the Church better off because she has given me her name? That I'm a Catholic? Am I living for the sake of the Church? Or is the Church existing for my well-being? Is this community of believers doing better because of the graces that I have for the Church? Are they more one, more unified because of me?

Another way that we have covered over our Sacraments of Matrimony is the way that we professionals have taken over teaching roles in the Church.

There is an instinctive distrust on our part of anybody who doesn't have clerical or religious credentials saying anything about the Church. We become conveyors of content to our people instead of lovers of them. An awful lot of times, we use our training and our education to control. Philosophy, theology, sociology, psychology, catechetics, and so forth can all provide beautiful insights and cast illumination on our pilgrimage. But pilgrimage is not fundamentally a wandering through theological or any like kind of by-ways.

We have to do a lot more listening to what our people are

experiencing in the faith and a lot less talking out about what they're supposed to be experiencing. This is true in all areas of the faith, but it's most especially true when it comes to our understanding of the Church itself.

Jesus did not say that the professionals should love the Church as he loves it, but he said that a husband should love his wife as he loves us. Yet we're constantly trying to tell the faithful what the Church is from our perspective of theology or catechetics or whatever and to a large degree, we have rendered invisible the sign of the Sacrament of Matrimony as a prophecy to the Church. We have been so vocal and pre-eminent that our couples are simply overlooked. It isn't even that we refuse to listen to them; it's that we don't even know that they have anything to say about the Church as couples. At best, we would listen to them as individual members of the Church. But in all likelihood only then if they talk to us on our terms with the equivalent of our background and our training.

What we have to start doing is to go to our couples and ask: "Tell us what you're experiencing in your relationship with one another and that will help us to begin to understand who all of us are as Church". Ecclesiology should begin with an experience of our sacramental couples. This teaching, of course, comes about not by their knowledge, not by their insightfulness about the facts of Church life, their awareness of the various professions, but strictly in terms of their relationship with one another and their relationship with us.

The fourth way in which we have covered over Matrimony and made the sign inaccessible is within our own fields of competence. We haven't had any serious study on the Sacrament of Matrimony. We haven't looked at the deep sacramentality of our couples.

We studied Canon Law; mainly in order to take care of divorce. And that's great. We are coming to have a compassionate heart. But that is not a study of the Sacrament of Matrimony. It's a study of what it's not — not what it is. What's happening here, of course, is that we're facing these couples from a pastoral point of view rather than a legal one and that's a tremendous step forward. We're dealing with them as flesh and blood people and trying to respond in tenderness and in love. We have a long way to go on this, but at least the process has begun. Furthermore, from a negative point of view we can get some tips and hints on what direction to look as far as developing a positive awareness of the Sacrament of Matrimony goes.

Once we start recognising the beauty of the comparison that the Lord uses in Scripture between his relationship with us, his people and the relationship between a husband and wife in the Sacrament of Matrimony, it most obviously is going to change our whole relationship with one another in the Church. It will tenderise us towards one another and help us to be much more personally involved.

But there is a very real bonus here. It also works the other way; it's going to help us to be much more understanding and much more sympathetic toward our couples. Just by the very fact that we start to see the interconnection between the two relationships, marital and ecclesial. Each will cast light upon the other. God teaches us through human means, but in the very use of those human means (in this case, the husband-wife relationship) to understand him better and his relationship with us, those human means become clarified in our minds and we have a much deeper appreciation and understanding of Matrimony as a love experience between a man and a woman.

We could, in fact, declare a moratorium on writing about the Church until our theologians go and sit with couples for a few years. Then they will have something powerful to say about the Church. I'm not trying to suggest that couples are technical theologians or would be able to speak the language of theologians. What they are capable of speaking is the language of a love relationship in the faith community. That's what being Catholic is at its core. There are all sorts of other things that being Catholic is, but they are all integrated into that one simple statement. Being immersed with sacramental couples will help our good professionals to approach the Church and their definitions of the Church from a totally different perspective. It will enable our catechists, our religious education people, our preachers and our teachers to use their skill, expertise and training with new insight and greater hope.

For it is only if our married people discover the differences in themselves from those who are not married and from those who are not married sacramentally that we are ever going to have the power to really change the Church and to be relevant to today's world. We can talk all we want about building community, but the basic core community in the world on any level you want to take it, sophisticated or most rudimentary, is that of the couple. All the great social engineering plans in the world and all the great good-will and all the grace for that matter is not going to be effective in building love communities among people unless we have the core community of the couple operating effectively, meaningfully and deeply with one another.

God knows, we have tried to build the fabric of Christendom and to recreate the unity that we so desperately desire within the community of believers. We have tried this in various ways for four centuries, and it just hasn't worked, because we really looked at things that had to be done. We have made all sorts of changes in our actions, and in principles, and in theologies, and in the formulation of propositions, in practices and habits that were held out as ideals for good, strong Catholic living.

All these have their place, of course, but they have to be in the context of relationships and love for one another. The ideal that was held out in the Acts of the Apostles still holds true today for the Church. The real norm by which the Church has to judge itself is how we love one another.

Unselfish love, however, goes against our whole inclination of life. We just don't want to be that dependent, that responsible to others. That's where the Sacrament of Matrimony comes in. Couples show us better than anybody else in human terms. They hold out a vision to us that first of all is possible to accomplish. True, unselfish love and finding my delight in the delight of the other person and finding my very identity in my relationship is a lived experience, not some kind of far-out ideal. So the best place to look to learn how to love is in the couple.

Do we really think our couples know this? Do we really believe that our sacramental couples have any comprehension that they are to provide the revelation of how the Church is to love one another and the Lord and how we are loved by the Lord? How

92

could they when there has been no catechesis for Matrimony? They haven't even *heard* their vocation.

But it's not just a question of neglect. We need to begin to recognise that our mentality towards our married couples in the Church is very much the mentality that we've had towards blacks and towards women. In other words, we recognise that we have been unfair to those of different races and to our women, that we haven't given them an opportunity to freely express their talents and their capabilities and their graces, so fortunately, thanks be to God, we have recently been actively seeking out opportunities for our women and other people who have suffered prejudice to come to the fore. We have to add the married to that category because certainly they have suffered a great deal of prejudice. Specifically as married. Celibates and professionals have almost a monopoly in leadership roles in the Church.

A very good thing to do just to help us to raise our consciousness would be that everytime we hear a statement about marriage or make one ourselves, or say something about husbands and wives, supposing we substituted the word "Jew" or the word "Black" in the statement that we were making. It would be very good discipline to do that and I think that it would be sharply surprising and relevatory for us just to see how prejudiced we are and how much we have to reform ourselves.

It isn't that we reject somebody because they happen to be married, but in our mind their marital status has nothing at all to do with positions that they may hold in the Church. We haven't up until this time seen their marriage as something we should actively look for, as something valuable and important, as their role in the Church. We haven't got across to them that their Sacrament enhances the whole Church. Our sacramental couples have a very low self image, specifically as couples. They believe they're in the Church to be taken care of. That the priests, brothers and sisters are the real Church. They simply do not see their love for one another as a vocation for the whole Church.

We've only recently introduced, or better reintroduced, the diaconate into the Church. The seriousness with which we take it is evidenced by the training that we demand. The resources that we expend on these men is impressive. In no way, shape or form

93

do we offer the same intensity of training for the Sacrament of Matrimony as we do for the Deacons. When married men receive the Diaconate, in fact, we call them Married Deacons. Maybe what we should be starting to do is call them "Deaconed Husbands" rather than married Deacons. As it is, married is merely a modification of deacon. And this is really because we see the Diaconate as affecting the Church directly. That being a deacon is really a Church experience and the focus is there, and we simply do not see our couples as being a Church experience in their coupleness.

So our couples have taken on the standard of non-Church couples for marriage. They have taken as the ideal of marriage what is held out as the norm for any marriage. They look on their marriage as a secular experience with some religious practices in the home. They accept the advice and direction of secular experts as perfectly suitable for their own relationship. This is not their fault; this is because of our abdication of our responsibility. We haven't offered them anything different. We fundamentally patted them on the hand and told them to go out and be a good married couple, to get along with one another and be happy.

And of course, even if we had offered them something different, they probably wouldn't have found too much help, because our spirituality is single-oriented, our morality is act-oriented and our faith credal.

7

UNCOVERING THE SIGNS

Now, there are some necessary things that we as a Church community, we as Catholics, have got to put into operation, so that our couples can become visible.

First of all, I believe that we, all of us, married, religious, priests, dedicated single people, have got to pray and do deep penance to rid ourselves of the heresy of individualism. This is so deeply ingrained that we don't even know how biased we are. It would be great to get somebody who is experienced in going through textbooks for sexism or racism, to go through even our Catholic school and CCD textbooks and see how biased we are against marriage and family relationship.

We're not even *aware* of how single-oriented we are, especially as priests and religious. How we deal with people as individuals and not as members of families; how we prioritise the values of independence, being right, freedom, self-identity over those of belonging, adapting to others, common goals. How frequently we support, if not directly foster, breeches in teen-parent relationships. How we have created a notion of community that is based on the attractiveness of common experiences, goals, understandings, preferences, rather than a community linked together beyond attraction. How we tend to value the opinions of those outside the faith community equally if not more so than those of our own people.

The fact of the matter is that we've been raised in an environment and atmosphere in which all the choices that are common wisdom are focused on personal fulfilment and individual satisfaction. That's why we've come to such conclusions as: young adults should move out of the home, the aged should live on their own or in a nursing home rather than in our own homes. We support those judgements. That's why we believe families should be small and each party to a marriage should be in it for what he or she gets out of it, and when the bottom line comes along, in almost all our decisions, in every area of our life, the relationship dimension gets sacrificed for the individual goals or satisfactions.

One of the real ministries to families is going to have to be a true conversion away from single values toward family values. The truth of the matter is that the Church is a family and not a collection of good singles. Therefore, anything we do to become more family oriented in our normal dealings with people is going to help us to become more aware of the Church itself and how we fit into God's plan. Unless people are experiencing in some depth the warmth and closeness of their human family it is going to be very difficult for them ever to see the Church as more than an institution or a group of do-gooders. This is not too harsh a saying or too strong a judgement.

In prayer let us ask our beloved Jesus just what our ambition is for the married. We can place the blame for the high level of marital failures that we're experiencing in the Church today on all sorts of extrinsic circumstances — and they do play a part. But one of the things that we're not looking at within ourselves is the part that *we* play. The truth is that most of us don't really expect too much of couples, we don't look on marriage as all that spiritual, we don't look on it as an essential element of the Church experience. So naturally, in the kind of Church environment that they're experiencing, there is very little support for high ambition, very little reward for good performance, very little ambition held out to them.

Another area that we have to look at is the training of our young people for the Sacrament of Matrimony. At best we train them for marriage. Anything that we can give them along the lines of human communication and responsiveness to each other is to be cheered. Nonetheless, they're not just getting married; they're getting matrimonied. And there is a whole catechesis of their relationship to the Church that's simply being ignored or taken strictly in terms of their individual personal relationship with God through the Church. When we do bring the Church in on our pre-marriage courses it's in terms of rules and regulations that are being imposed by the institutional Church, most specifically in terms of the ceremony with some further reference to the morality of marriage when it comes to children and divorce. The institutional dimensions of the Sacrament of Matrimony are entirely too much to the fore.

Our training gets across to them the mentality that the Church is taking care of them. The Church is giving them something. The Church is watching over them as a good mother and is rooting for them to do well with one another. All that is very well and good, but it's very maternalistic. Even more importantly, it really misses the whole point of the Sacrament of Matrimony. It is simply not getting across the idea that their love for one another in the Church is a vocation from and for the whole Church. And that they have a real mission to the whole Church through their sacramental relationship.

Another thing we need to do is find the ways to live out the call of Vatican II to develop the ministry of the married to married, of family to family. We have a social worker mentality towards service in the Church rather than a sacramental one. We look on the Sacraments as nice and important on a personal level, but when it comes to putting people in charge of apostolates within the Church we look for more "serious" qualifications. We would never think of saying: "Well now, in the family life office, we should get the couple who is best living out the Sacrament of Matrimony." We look and see what college they went to, what degrees they have, what experience in the "field". Yet they are secondary things compared with the qualifications of the Sacrament. What we've got to do is decide: do we want to have really outstanding Sacraments of Matrimony providing real leadership in the Church, most especially in the areas of Family Life? If we really want them, then we will develop ways to discern who is called to serve the Church in this way.

We've got to start recruiting the Sacrament of Matrimony just like we recruit for the Sacrament of Priesthood and for religious life. And match-making is a part of it. If we discover that we know a young lady who's beautiful and good and faithful and we happen to know a young man who's strong in the faith and a good person, I think if we really believe in the Sacrament of Matrimony, we'll

97

introduce them to one another. That's one of the tests of how much I believe in marriage as a Sacrament: do I match-make? As sisters and as priests, one of the beautiful things that maybe we've lost in recent years is that we used to recruit very strongly for our Orders and for our seminaries. The reason that we've stopped doing that is that we question whether anybody can be happy there, and that's the reason why parents are resisting vocations to the priesthood and religious life in their children. But, they'll make the same mistake with the Sacrament of Matrimony. We complain about the young person's choice, and we complain about the mixed-marriage rate. But we havn't done anything for those kids. We've let them make rotten choices and then we say, "See, it's a rotten choice!" That's not good enough.

One of the beautiful things that we had, and still to some degree have, is the reverence people have for priests and religious. Yes, sometimes it was superstitious and not coming from the proper motivation. But that reverence led many priests and religious to live out the call that was theirs in much better ways and with much more generosity. Taking our priests and religious for granted is not improving the situation at all. Treating them just like anybody else in the Church is not any plus factor either. And as far as our couples are concerned, too, we haven't treated their marriages as anything special. Everyone in the Church, married or single, priest, religious, or lay is going to have to start to develop a real awe of the Sacrament of Matrimony — our couples. We have to reverence our couples. That's got to be the first stage in our catechesis of Matrimony.

We can imagine how difficult it would be for our young people to believe that Jesus Christ is present under the appearance of bread and wine if we were to treat that Sacrament the same way we treat the Sacrament of Matrimony. Truly in a very real way we have to accuse ourselves of sacrilege when it comes to Matrimony. We have been treating a holy thing carelessly and profanely. Not just those who engage in it, but all of us in the Church. The reverence for Matrimony we are talking about here cannot restrict itself strictly and solely to the occasion of the wedding, nor can it just be a celebration of the 25th wedding anniversary or the 50th. In reality that just gives testimony to our wonder at the long-suffering of this couple. Either their physical endurance in living that long or their spiritual endurance in being able to put up with one another for that period of time. We indicate a certain being surprised.

Nor can we merely express our reverence by having a special feast day for our couples once a year. It has to be a day-in day-out practical reverence by the whole community of believers for this special Sacrament which is in their midst.

One of the questions to ask ourselves is just how much attention we pay to our couples. Part of our difficulty is that we really do believe that we are spending time with our married people. After all, they make up the majority of the adults who are in Church on Sunday. It is their children whom we teach in school and in CCD. It is they who are in our parish organisations. But we are *not* dealing with them in terms of their marriage. We have the mistaken belief that if they become better people, they are automatically going to become better as far as their marriage is concerned.

Do we as teachers in our Catholic schools or in our CCD classes take as a personal responsibility the developing and promoting of the marriages of the parents of our pupils? For the life the parents are leading really determines how open to grace those children are. It is the love they experience in their home that disposes them for the love of Jesus.

Just from the point of view of our concern for those kids, we have to involve ourselves in the life of their parents, not just to visit the parents to encourage them to get the kids to work harder or to pay more attention to us or to be more disciplined in class. But to visit the parents for the sake of the parents' own relationship with one another, to take on as part of our ministry to the kids a real ministry to the couple. Not specifically as parents but as married. That's more important than anything that we directly tell our children or show our children through our own love. It seems to me that part of the curriculum of any school (whether CCD or Catholic school) has got to be a very definite, continuous, frequent involvement with the couple as a couple.

Moreover, do we choose as teachers of the Sacrament of Matrimony in our schools or in our CCD classes the best married couples we know? Marriage is a charism in the Church and charism has got to be exposed. Do we let our married couples show and share their experiences instead of teaching Matrimony as a subject? We have to recognise that the Sacrament is always enfleshed. It's always a couple; it's not something out there. If we're really going to teach the Sacrament of Matrimony, we have to expose them to sacramental couples and not just to theories or practices or conclusions.

If we are really serious about our Sacraments of Matrimony, we have got to be concerned, too, about conversion experiences. Bishop Bernadine said, when he was President of the National Conference of Catholic Bishops: "What the Church needs today, what Catholics need today are conversion experiences". And there are conversion experiences that are focused on the Sacraments of Matrimony. And the most obvious one by far is Marriage Encounter.

All too often, people in the Church say: "Married people are taking care of that". But we have no right to shove Marriage Encounter off into the corner like that. It should be our personal responsibility to make sure that every married couple we know makes a Marriage Encounter. You say: "I don't know if I agree with it". You don't have to agree with it. Let the couples decide. The fact is that Marriage Encounter has proved to be a true conversion experience, both on the human level in their relationship to one another, and on the spiritual level in their relationship to the Church. We are simply in no position to say that's not going to happen to this specific couple. I may not like the way it's accomplished, I may have other favourite occasions for grace in the Church than Marriage Encounter, but nonetheless, Marriage Encounter (whether I like it or not) has been a very real moment of loving grace for hundreds of thousands of couples in the Church. Therefore, not only do I have no right to oppose it, I have a positive obligation to foster it among all those couples whose lives I touch.

As professional leaders in the Church, we tend to stand off in judgement. It has to be on our terms and our way. Unless we agree with something and we like something or we're pleased by the way people approach us about it, then we just sit on it and if we don't positively clamp down on it we don't feel any responsibility to get things moving.

It's like the old dumb stuff between Religious Orders where if I was a Jesuit the only thing that really counted was the Sodality, and the Third Order of St. Francis was second class stuff. That was stupid. Sure, I have a particular predilection for the beauty of the spiritual exercises that St. Ignatius offers, but I can't be blind to the multiple charisms that are in the Church and the diversity of the spiritualities that are available within our faith family. So it can't be just that I don't say anything in public against the Third Order of Carmelites or what have you, but I have to positively foster an awareness in my people and an encouragement in my people to test it out. We have no right to make decisions for other people. If I don't offer them some knowledge of what is available, I am making a negative decision for them.

It should be a personal responsibility of anybody who has any influence in the parish to make sure that our couples have the best possible shot at living up to their sacramental way of life. We can't sit down and say: "Well, I hope somebody gets to them". If you know them, it's the Lord's call for *you* to get to them. Our ambition for our couples has got to be visible.

Another factor that we have to consider seriously here is the importance of building up a sense of solidarity among the people of sacramental marriages. We have heard about the solidarity of the working class, that they have common visions and common goals and common needs and common problems and common desires. The same thing has got to be true of married people within the Church. There is an important value in the community of the married.

The difficulty is that we haven't distinguished our married couples from any other lay people. We have left each individual couple as an isolated marital unit existing on its own. It simply doesn't work well that way. What we have now is wives talking to wives, husbands doing some degree of talking with husbands. We don't really have couples who are fully committed to being sacramental, discussing with and probing with one another in order to increase their potential to be real lovers in their Sacraments. We are going to have to build associations of married people speci-

101

fically as married to get them talking about their potential and their possibilities, to support them in their difficulties and to be able to speak in their name. This solidarity, of course, has to be specifically among the *sacramentally* married. Otherwise the values we will be achieving will be at best diverse ones if not completely distorted ones.

We personally should look for, recognise and congratulate those couples who have good marriages. You know, one of the things that I think we recognise is that it is often very lonely being a priest in a pulpit, because so often he finishes and nobody says anything. It's nice for somebody to come up after a Mass and say: "Father, that really meant something to me". It's kind of lonely being a Sister and teaching day after day in a grade school, or working in a hospital, or working as a social worker. And nobody pays any attention to them as Sisters; they're just teachers, or they're doing a great job with the poor. And nobody ever says: "You know, you're a great person, but even more, you're a Sister; thank you for being a Sister for us!" And I think that, just like the couples should go after Mass and see the priest, I think that people should go after Mass and see the couples and say: "You have a great thing going for you and for us — and thank you". That "thank you" is very important in order to get across to our people who are in the Sacrament of Matrimony that their relationship with one another makes our life better. That we're more of a priest or Sister or Catholic and the Church is more itself because of their sacramental relationship.

The homily at the Eucharist should more frequently focus on growth in marriage and not just on the problems and on parenthood. One of the complaints is: "Well, it's all on marriage". There's almost nothing on marriage from the pulpit. There's a fair amount on family life, thanks be to God. But we're trying to be so democratic we want to write homilies that fit everybody. We simply can't. That comes out as a bland nothing.

That doesn't mean that we should speak to just one group in the Church all the time. But we should definitely speak to the major groups in the Church frequently. There are at least 57 times during the course of the year when all our people are together for Mass. So we have plenty of opportunities to speak individually to

groups of people. The divorced and separated should be specifically addressed, not just for their sake, but for the sake of the
whole community in the parish, so that they are recognised as a
vibrant part of this parish and so that our people who are in other
categories of faith experience recognise them and respond to
them. The same thing is true as far as widows, single young adults
and the married are concerned.

At Baptism we should formally recognise it as the Sacrament of
Matrimony being proclaimed. That it is those parents and their
love for one another as a Sacrament that is permitting us to have
this Sacrament and not just something we're doing for the child.
Sometimes it just seems at the Sacrament of Baptism that the
parents are positively irrelevant. Oh sure, they produce the child,
but that's as far as it goes. Whatever remarks we address to the
group in attendance, whatever explanation we give at the ceremony is really not complete unless we pay due homage to the
Sacrament of Matrimony — that couple. It is their love for one
another that has made this occasion possible. The Sacrament of
Matrimony is being celebrated every time there is a Baptism and
we should take formal public note of that reality.

The parish newsletter should carry regular articles on marriage.

I hope that our Charismatic brothers and sisters will begin to
encourage prayer in accordance with all the Sacraments and not
just the Sacrament of Baptism. People should pray as religious, as
priests, as married, and they should not all say the same prayer or
the same style of prayer. It is a very important obligation on the
part of our Charismatic brothers and sisters to start to call couples
to be couples in that prayer and not just to let them pray as
individuals. Jesus himself has differentiated the way that he deals
with us through the Sacraments. So we can't deny his choice of
a sacramental relationship and just have him treating us all identi-
cally so that our response to him is the same.

The extreme of this, of course, is in a situation where the
husband or wife is actually separated from the spouse by their
relationship with a prayer group. It seems to me very dubious at
best, that someone who is married can be called to a relationship
with Jesus that is apart from, if not divisive of the relationship
between husband and wife. Sometimes what happens in these

circumstances is that it builds in superiority on the part of one spouse toward the other on the basis of their relationship with Jesus. Oh, it's expressed in very gentle terms and very, very sweetly, but the superiority can be sickening! "He's not ready yet". "I'm praying very hard for her". "I'm using my relationship with the Lord to love him more". Actually, the husband or wife's relationship with their spouse is much more likely to be a witness of Jesus' presence in this world than my relationship directly with Jesus.

The Sacrament of Matrimony is a charism that should be celebrated in our prayer groups. In the Charismatic movement — which is beautiful and important to the whole well-being of the Church — our couples should be instructed that their finding of the Lord should all lead them to improve their whole life — and I don't care how well they pray; if they can't talk to their husbands, it's no good. They have to be made to realise that the Lord will not be satisfied until their husband or their wife is part of their relationship with him. We can't leave it as something separate.

Sometimes a person's intimacy with the Lord is shared much more openly and much more frequently with people in a prayer group than it is with his wife or husband. That is a serious loss to their marriage and it should not be encouraged. So what a spouse should be talking about with brothers and sisters in a prayer group is not where the spouse is failing by not accepting Jesus and not just where I'm developing or lacking in development as far as my prayer life is concerned. What I have to be talking about with my brothers and sisters is: "What is the flaw in me and in the way I'm expressing my love for my husband or wife that is blocking out Jesus from my spouse?" Because that's the reality.

If my relationship with Jesus is all that real and all that attractive, and if my relationship with my wife or with my husband is that meaningful, then my spouse will not resist. The basic problem is not that he's resisting Jesus, it's that he's resisting his wife because he's not experiencing the love that he believes he should be experiencing. The cure of this problem is not in terms of a deeper prayer life on the part of either of them. It's a deeper love life. Once that is accomplished, then the barriers to Jesus will soon come down.

104

I don't believe that the Lord separates couples. It's very difficult for me to understand how anybody can be accepted for Baptism in the Spirit in their marriage without their spouse. The answer to that, of course, is, "Well the Lord treats us individually". And that's the whole point at issue — I don't think he does. I think he treats us in terms of our love relationships. He has called us to be a couple. He's not going to deny his call. He has said that the two of us are to be two in one flesh. I don't think he calls us to be two in one flesh and then to be separate in the Spirit.

There are serious reformations that have to be made in our whole approach to people in preaching the Gospel message. Parish or societies should not split husband and wife. Full-time personnel should have a close personal tie with couples on an individual love relationship basis, and those couples should have a strong influence on the ministry of that Sister or layperson or priest and on their relationship with different parishioners. The relationships that our priests and Sisters and dedicated laity have tend to be with single persons or with married persons who are separated from their spouse in the activity that they're engaging in in the parish. The point that we're focusing on here is not the loss that is to the apostolate in itself, although it certainly is. But what we're talking about is the loss to the priest or Sister. They're simply not being exposed to one of the major charisms in the Church for their own personal growth and development.

We all need to develop a conscious dependence upon the success and generosity of our couples in their relationship with one another for our own spiritual life. It is very clear that if the level of spirituality of priests is low then the whole Church is going to suffer. So too, if the level of love between husbands and wives in sacramental marriages is low, then the whole Church is deprived. For in all of us human beings the action has to be in our lived experience. God can't be someone who is acting outside of us, even though his actions are wonderfilled. He has to be someone who is living in our midst. That is the Incarnation. He pitched his tent among us. We need to be experiencing him, not just to know *about* him.

And the Sacrament of Matrimony responds to that need. If a man actually does love his wife as he loves his own body, if a woman is fully responsive to her husband, if they do those things as a calling from the Lord in the Church, then those words are not abstractions any more. They are flesh and blood realities which really touch us. If we let them. If we listen to them.

We as priests and religious have simply got to recognise that sacramental couples are like prayers, spiritual reading and the other Sacraments in the Church. They are necessary means for our growth in our own vocation. So we just can't read up on marriage. We have to be exposed to a living Sacrament — the couple.

It would be good also to establish on a parish and a diocesan level a council of the Sacrament of Matrimony — in other words a council of couples who would be a visionary and prophetic voice speaking to the ministry of how Matrimony reveals Jesus' relationship with these faithful people we call the Church. The point of this would be to give our couples a voice. Not just to give them their say in making the decisions that affect the life of the parish, although that certainly would be invaluable in itself, but even more than that, to let them set the tone. It isn't the pragmatic decision so much as the whole direction. The whole vision of who we are called to be to one another that comes out of their experience of the Sacrament of Matrimony — it should be their voice that is dominant in establishing the community dimension of the parish.

On a monthly basis, we should have communal penance services in our parishes to make reparation for the desecration that is poured out over our Sacrament of Matrimony, for the desecration that our couples endure at the hands of the media. To say nothing of the disrespect that we personally express through our jokes and puns about marriage, and the sins on the part of married people themselves in the way they sometimes treat one another. The Pioneers were founded to do reparation for the abuse of alcohol; Forty Hours Devotion was instituted to make up for the irreverence with which the Eucharist was treated. Today's profanity and sacrilege is against the Sacrament of Matrimony. We simply would not tolerate the open contempt and careless irreverence that is so prevalent in our society towards the Sacrament of Matrimony, if it was expressed towards the Eucharist.

Maybe we're not too moved by this. Maybe we don't think that this is a pressing urgency. There are so many other things in the

Church that need changing. But just stop and think of living in an anti-clerical society where the hostility to priesthood is institutionalised, where it's just taken for granted. When we live in a society like that, what happens? First of all, vocations are sharply reduced. Secondly, and worse, the relationship between priests and people is one of suspicion and distance. But we live in an anti-marital society in our Church. That is not too strong a term. We really do.

Even from the pulpit we can make sly little remarks about marriage, or little jokes. We can allow horribly vicious statements to be made about parents in our teachers' rooms and sometimes even overtly in mothers' club meetings. We can treat the Sacrament of Matrimony as a matter of total irrelevance when it comes to running a parish. So even if we're highly enlightened and we sincerely and honestly want to bring the lay people into full-fledged partnership so that the co-ministry includes the whole Church, even then it's simply in terms of a baptismal ministry. We don't recognise at all that the matrimonied have a totally different charism and that their voice has to be heard specifically as matrimonied. So we very definitely have to do penance and we have to raise the consciousness in ourselves and in our people of how carelessly and how irreverently we have acted toward our matrimonied couples.

Of course, the whole parish should be present at this communal penance. It's not just for the married. The married have their sins against the Sacraments to reconcile for. First of all, in the way they have failed with one another, and secondly, in the way they have supported the negative environment toward Matrimony. But each one of us is responsible in the parish. Priests, Sisters, young, old, single, widowed, divorced, married.

A tremendous catechesis could develop out of this kind of thing. It can't be a canned-type of ceremony, it just can't be a formal prayer type of thing. It calls for personal witness that can be done anonymously by submitting something in writing, or it can be done by personal presence, but the fact of the matter is, that if we are just penitential in our own heart, it's not enough. There has to be a witness to our penance.

Maybe we are ill-at-ease and even hostile towards some of these suggestions. It just shows how unimportant Matrimony is in our minds and hearts. We do not see our couples as sacred; we have taken on the wisdom of this world rather than that of Jesus.

Another essential task is to search out the young married in our parishes or schools to support, encourage and call them forth to grace. We have to have a special tenderness in our hearts for those who are just beginning their love for one another and for us in the Sacrament of Matrimony. Too often, we give them a pre-marriage course, we go through the wedding ceremony, and then we just back off from them until they come to us with a problem in their marriage. Or until they have to go to the tribunal to get an annulment. Or, at best, until they come to us to put a child in the school.

We have to have a carefully defined and worked out plan first of all to identify the newly marrieds that are moving into the parish and then develop contact with them, to make them feel involved. It can't just be visiting them once and blessing their homes. That's nice — it's a good start — but we have to go much deeper than that. We have to introduce them to other good marriages and encourage them to build a close personal relationship with older, more experienced sacramental couples as well as with their own age group. We have to offer them further opportunities to grow by providing programmes that are specifically geared for them in their Sacrament.

Have a monthly Mass to celebrate the Sacrament of Matrimony, rejoicing in the couples in your midst, in your parish. "Oh my God, we can't do that, if we don't do it for the others!" Well, first of all even in the smallest of parishes there are at least eight Masses a month if you count Saturday evening and Sunday alone. So there's room for everybody. Secondly, the Sacrament of Matrimony is special. All those other groups deserve well of the Church but the St. Vincent de Paul Society, or Altar and Rosary Societies, or whatever, are not Sacraments. We should have nothing but the greatest reverence for the St. Vincent de Paul Society. The St. Vincent de Paul Society is a very precious group of men and women, hopefully of couples, who are really concerned about the poor in the parish, and they have borne the heat of the day with very little support and very little help. But they are not a Sacra-

ment — neither are the Charismatics; neither are Marriage Encounter; neither are the divorced. Now all of those, I think, should
be reached out to. But Matrimony is one of the seven Sacraments
in the Church. At best, we've reduced the Sacrament to the level
of a society or an organisation!

Our Sacramental couples should take part in any renewal pro-
gramme that we have in our diocese for Priests and Sisters. The
charism of Matrimony is an important gift for these vocations.
I do not believe that we Priests or Sisters will ever understand the
Church until we get close to our couples. One of the reasons why
we get bitter and unhappy and are very withdrawn is because we
are not close to couples. We become awfully narrow and restricted
that way and our own personal concerns loom too large in our
vision of the Church. We need the salt of our married couples to
give us the true savour of the Church. And so that our own way of
life will be richer, more meaningful and more in accordance with
the Gospel message.

It's funny that never has celibacy been under so much attack
or provided so much of a painful difficulty for so many good
religious and priests. At least in our memory. And the reason is
not so much because marriage seems so attractive, but that celibacy
seems so burdensome. And that singleness seems so attractive.
Actually, the more we talk to one another the more unattractive
celibacy is going to appear to be. We're going to be bringing out to
one another our difficulties with it. On the other hand, in relationship to our couples, the Sacrament of Matrimony, our devotion
to celibacy is going to increase and expand. They have an awareness of the beauty of our life experience that we don't have for
ourselves.

What's interesting to note, by the way, is that the Sacrament of
Matrimony and the broad scale practice of celibacy came into the
Church at approximately the same time. Furthermore, it is only
those Churches that practise and revere celibacy that recognise
Matrimony as a Sacrament. Those two realities are very definitely
inter-connecting. It is not an accident. We very much do have a
stake in one another; we belong to one another, and we reinforce
one another by the various lives of love that we have chosen. So

109

we need a real exposure to matrimonied couples in order to appreciate our own sacramental and religious experience.

Yes, we need a real exposure to matrimonied couples. For they are a sign of us Catholics; the key to our whole discovery of ourselves as Church; the parable of how Jesus loves the Church.